T0193939

God Is an Elephant in Orthopedic Shoes

A Memoir in Four Part Harmony

BRAD CENTER

authorHOUSE®

AuthorHouse™
1663 Liberty Drive
Bloomington, IN 47403
www.authorhouse.com
Phone: 1 (800) 839-8640

Published by AuthorHouse 11/06/2017

ISBN: 978-1-5462-1183-9 (sc)
ISBN: 978-1-5462-1181-5 (hc)
ISBN: 978-1-5462-1182-2 (e)

Library of Congress Control Number: 2017915349

Print information available on the last page.

Any people depicted in stock imagery provided by Thinkstock are models,
and such images are being used for illustrative purposes only.
Certain stock imagery © Thinkstock.

This book is printed on acid-free paper.

CONTENTS

FOREWORD

Whether I shall turn out to be the hero of my own life, or whether that station will be held by anybody else, these pages must show…

Charles Dickens, *David Copperfield*

INTRODUCTION

Memory is a fragile thing. Imagine soap bubbles gently hovering above a bed of nails. It's that kind of fragile. We look back on our lives with a strong belief in the accuracy of our memories and in the events unfolded therein. In truth, we should doubt the accuracy of any long-ago memory; but it is all that we have – these attenuated wisps of truth. So, I will take these wisps, these vapors, these loose embodiments of fact, and swirl them around and then we will see what will come out from behind the mist.

On these pages, I will attempt to pin down memories of a life that has been well spent so far and with much more to come – at least this is my hope. Whether these musings have much meaning outside of those lives I have touched, I cannot say, but for me and those I have come to know and care about, I hope it will bring a mixture of joy, laughter, surprises and some modicum of insight.

Acknowledgments

I have three "voices" to thank before I begin. First, my mother who inspires me because she (as only a mother can) believes in the very best I have to offer. Secondly, I must thank my wife and my love, Valerie, who makes each day more meaningful. Finally, a thank you to my friend Richard Kosoff, who travelled this road before me and produced an "accounting" of his life, therefore challenging me to do the same.

Contributions

I want to thank Linda Kosoff for the cover of this book and her interpretation of my strange title. I also want to thank Dara Light and Nicole Kosoff for their editing skills because no matter how many times I revise and review my own work, I always miss something. Lastly, I want to thank all the people named and unnamed whose actions, reactions, and memories have become integral to the stories that are my life.

INTRODUCTION PART II

As I began to formulate the contents of this book, I had a bit of a revelation. Because this book is truly mine, I can put any damn thing into it that I want! Therefore, I have decided to include not only the stories and anecdotes of my past but other material that I wanted to share. This material includes some philosophical musings, some top-ten lists, some poetry and fiction, and just about any other darn thing that strikes my fancy. All of these things are important aspects of who I am, and if this book is meant to do anything, it is meant to provide some context to my life. So, my "fellow traveler," beware. The road ahead is filled with strange and odd little detours.

PART 1

Out of Time (Ok, this is kind of, sort of, maybe still, a bit of an introduction but it's important)

A Note About the Title

You might be wondering about the title of this book. Is there some deep meaning that lies beneath this odd title? Does the title give some insight into my character? Does it reveal some mystery into the meaning of the universe? Unfortunately, the answer to each of these questions is no. Here's the story…

I recently had a strange dream (something that happens quite often) and awoke to tell my wife all about it. I didn't have all the elements of the dream clear in my head but somehow, while the details of the dream were fuzzy, the dream had a very specific title: *God is an Elephant in Orthopedic Shoes*. I knew that God and elephants were well represented in the dream but, as I said, things were fuzzy except for the title. God as an elephant! I know, that's kind of odd or blasphemous (if you are the type of person who thinks in those terms) but I guess there are stranger ideas out there. However, I will admit this one's a little weird.

I turned to my wife and told her the title of the dream. My wife politely informed me that dreams don't have titles. "They're just dreams!" she said.

1

I agreed on general principle, but there I was shaking my head all the same. The dream was *God is an Elephant in Orthopedic Shoes* – no discussion.

She said (again politely), "Nobody names their dreams."

I told her that I didn't intentionally name it, but that was just the name that seemed to come with it. Like an item on the menu, my subconscious mind just seemed to select the appropriate title. It was in my head, what could I say? So, I figured, what the hell, let's roll with it. The title of this book must be "God is an Elephant in Orthopedic Shoes". Will I discuss God or elephants? Who's to say for sure? Turn the page and see for yourself.

PART 2

In the Beginning…

"It's partly true, too, but it isn't all true. People always think something's all true."
J.D. Salinger – *The Catcher in the Rye*

Tranquility Base

The first memory I have is at three years old – or at least I think it was about that age (soap bubbles, remember?). I was in this little pool behind the house gliding around gently and smoothly. Why the heck do I remember that particular moment? I have no idea. Is this moment important in the grand scheme of my life? I kind of doubt it. While I have always enjoyed the water, and I was a pretty good swimmer, it was never a great factor in my life. Sorry for leading anyone to believe this had some cosmic foreshadowing that I would become an Olympic swimmer. I am afraid that just never happened. What I do recall was a feeling of utter tranquility. Can a three-year-old truly comprehend or apprehend a feeling of tranquility? Well, I guess probably not, but that is the feeling that comes to me now as I evoke the memory. I look back on that day from time to time. I take out the memory, caress it and hold it gently in my mind. It is a good one.

PART 3

Getting to the Good Stuff First

Ted Kennedy Saves My Life

I'm 26. I know what you're thinking: What the hell happened to years four through 25? I never promised I was going to go strictly in chronological order. I do promise, however, to circle back, but I have a several good stories to tell and I don't want your attention to wander. Let's begin with a classic little tale I like to call "Ted Kennedy Saved My Life." I know that sounds a bit melodramatic, and I suppose it is, but see what you think.

Here's the deal. I am living in Virginia and working on Capitol Hill as a Legislative Assistant to Senator Arlen Specter. When you first start on the Hill, they brief you on proper Hill etiquette. You need to follow certain rules and they go something like this:

Rule #1 – There are certain elevators that are for Senators only. You can only ride in one if you are in the company of a Senator.

Rule #2 – There is a tram that runs from the Senate office buildings to the Capitol. The front car of each tram is reserved for Senators only.

Rule #3 – You cannot enter onto the Senate floor unless you are wearing a suit jacket.

Being new to the Hill and not wanting to screw up too badly, I took the lessons to heart, but maybe just a bit too much to heart, as you will now see.

It's somewhere around the middle of my first week and I am off to the Capitol from the Senate Hart Office Building. I am comfortably seated in the second car of the tram (see Rule #2) and I am waiting for it to depart. Out of the corner of my eye I see a short older woman approach and then seat herself in the first car. Alarm bells start going off in my head. This poor woman doesn't know the rules! The gentleman operating the tram is looking elsewhere and I am in a bit of a panic regarding the plight of this obviously ill-informed and confused woman. I quickly start rehearsing how I am going to gently, politely, but firmly tell her that she needs to get out of the first tram car, as it is reserved for senators only. I am working up the nerve and my hand is reaching out to tap her on the shoulder. My mouth is beginning to form the words and then I hear the unmistakable voice of Senator Ted Kennedy. He is walking down to the tram car at a good clip. He shouts, "Barbara, Barbara, hold the tram. I need to talk to you." He sits down next to the woman. I pull back my hand, oh so quickly and quietly. Realization dawns on me that the "little older woman" is in fact Senator Barbara Mikulski from Maryland.

Let me make something very clear at this juncture. Senator Mikulski is not someone you trifle with. She is one tough lady. If Ted Kennedy had not walked in at that moment, and had I succeeded in my ill-conceived plan, requesting that Senator Mikulski leave the front of the tram, I would have had my ass neatly handed to me in short order. I would have had the shortest Legislative Assistant career in Capitol Hill history. Perhaps it is melodramatic to say Ted Kennedy saved my life just then, but it felt like it.

A quick, personal note on Senator Kennedy: He had a long a distinguished career as a U.S. Senator and the following comment is not meant to diminish that career in any way shape or form and (as I just pointed out) he saved my life, but I must say this – I have never seen a person with a larger head in all my life. I am not speaking metaphorically about his ego; I am talking about the actual size of the man's head. It was huge. We are talking a T-Rex sized head sitting on a normal man's shoulders. I know he is no longer with us and I mean no disrespect but this was a simple biological fact. It was a huge head! Sorry but it was huge – really!

Senator Orin Hatch Steals My Coat

I am still 26, and it's time for another Capitol Hill story. It's another normal day up on the Hill (although there really aren't very many normal days). There's a vote scheduled late that evening, and I am waiting for Senator Specter by the entrance to the Senate Chamber. Specter is out for dinner, so I strategically stake out a place in front of the Senate Chamber so I can brief him before he enters the Chamber for a vote.

I should add that is not a critically important vote. It has something to do with some parcel of land in North Carolina being designated as a national refuge. Suffice it to say that the fate of western civilization does not hang in the balance. It is a totally noncontroversial vote and is sure to pass, but I need to give Specter the details before he walks on the floor. I should add that I've been working on the Hill for only four months, so this is all relatively new to me and briefing Specter is downright stressful for me. I have one goal in mind: don't mess it up. Specter is a former prosecuting attorney and tends to act like it. He asks probing questions and they come out fast. He wants detailed and well thought-out answers. He likes testing you to see if you are smart enough.

So, I am standing by the entrance to the Senate waiting for Senator Specter to come back from dinner when I spot him coming into the building. I proceed to tell him the expected vote count and the specifics of the bill, etc. At this juncture, my back is to the Senate Chamber as I brief the Senator. Suddenly, in the midst of briefing Specter, I get this tap on my shoulder, and I hear a voice behind me say, "I need your coat." I hear nothing more and nothing less. I am not turning my back on the Senator in the middle of my briefing to address some idiot who, for reasons unknown to me, wants my suit jacket.

So, I don't turn my back to Specter to see why someone is asking for my coat and continue with my briefing. Specter says nothing. He gives nothing away. His face and overall demeanor remain unchanged, so I continue. Another ten or fifteen seconds pass, and once again I hear a plea for my coat – this time a little more urgently. Again, I do not turn around and stoically press on. Specter still says nothing, like there is nothing going on behind me. I figure, if he isn't going to acknowledge the weirdo behind me, then I won't either. I continue the briefing.

Another five seconds or so pass and again I hear the voice and this time it is not a plea but a demand. I hear, "I need your coat, now!"

Before I can respond, Specter, says, "Uh Brad, I believe Senator Hatch would like to borrow your coat."

I turn, and there is Senator Orin Hatch standing impatiently behind me dressed in a God-awful outfit: green pants and some green and white polo shirt. He looked like a pool table had vomited on him. I give him my coat, finally catching on to what was going on. Apparently, Hatch had come in from the golf course or wherever and needed to get on to the floor of the Senate for the vote, but he could not get onto the floor because he didn't have a jacket on. Senate rules forbid any man from being on the Senate floor unless he has on a suit jacket – well-known senator or not.

Hatch must have sized me up quickly and figured my coat would fit him. I am around six feet, four inches tall, and he is just a couple inches shorter. I hand Hatch the coat and he walks into the Senate Chamber. I then proceed to wait. Specter comes and goes after the vote but Hatch remains inside. I wait for about two hours for him to come out. I am just standing there twiddling my thumbs. This is way before smartphones, and I have literally nothing to do.

Now here comes the kicker. He finally comes out of the Chamber, flanked by a couple of his staffers, and he walks right by me with my coat still on his back. What am I going to do? What can I do? I chase him down. I tap him on the shoulder and ask for my coat back. He looks at me for a few seconds, trying to place just who the hell I am, and suddenly it dawns on him that he is still wearing my coat. He takes it off and says a quick thank you. Like I said, there was no such thing as a normal day up there.

I Single-Handedly Insult the Nation of South Korea

I'm 25 and serving as a management analyst at the Pentagon. Being pretty low in the office hierarchy, I am by no means doing anything truly important. One morning, I am asked to go out to the "South Parking" and meet a general from South Korea and escort him up to the office. I turn to my boss and ask, "Is there anything I need to know?"

My boss says, "No, just meet him in the parking lot and bring him up." I walk down to the entrance and wait for the general and his entourage to come into the building. I wait for about five or ten minutes and nothing – no general, no entourage, zilch. Eventually, I get a little anxious and go outside to scan the parking lot. A Korean officer sees me scanning the parking lot and approaches me. He correctly guesses that I am their escort, and indicates that his group has been denied parking in the lot because they do not have a parking pass. The officer I am with is not the general. The general is back in the car waiting and he is not a happy camper.

You're kidding me, I think. *This is not happening.* I walk back to the guard's desk inside and explain the situation. I tell him we have an unhappy Korean general just outside the parking lot, and I absolutely must get him up to our offices ASAP, so please help me avoid an international incident and let him and his team park their damn car! The guard hands me a pass and tells me to calm down. "Bring him in," he says.

I walk with the other Korean officer (who I figure is something like a captain) to the car to escort them in. At this point, I begin to notice how nervous and uncomfortable the captain seems to be. His English is limited, and I decide not to pry, but now I am beginning to feel a little uncomfortable myself. When we get to the car, the general and the rest of his team are dead silent. I get them into the parking lot and to one of the guest spots with no additional issues. The general then gets out of the car and walks quietly to a small embankment at the edge of the parking lot. He crosses his arms in front of his chest and turns away from me.

I turn back to the captain, who is now noticeably sweating. "What the heck is going on?" I say. I look at the captain, he stares back at me and says nothing. I think he is too scared to speak. I can tell I am on my own. I tell the captain that we can go in now – no issues. The captain, gathering his courage, walks up to me slowly and in a hushed tone, he tells me that we (I am guessing we means the entire United States Army) have insulted the general by not adequately preparing for his visit.

I apologize. What else can I do? I tell him how sorry I am and that I had simply been asked to bring him in and that I had no idea things were not ready for their arrival. As I do this, I begin to imagine tomorrow's *Washington Post* headline: "South Korea Breaks off Diplomatic Relations with the US – Unnamed Pentagon Staffer said to be the Cause."

I spend five minutes pleading with the captain and looking up at the general but nothing is moving this man. He is an unmoving granite slab. He is the Rock of Gibraltar. He has been insulted and is not going in, period. Eventually, I nod, hang my head and leave. There is nothing else I can do.

I walk back into the Pentagon trying to figure out how to explain to my boss, who was fairly high up in the food chain, just how I had screwed this up. My boss takes it rather well, all things considered. He tells me it is not my fault. I tend to agree but say nothing. He also indicates that he will arrange for a follow-up meeting with the general and his team. I ask him if someone else might be responsible for escorting him into the Pentagon. He smiles and nods in agreement.

PART 4

"Pre-History" or "A Rose by Any Other Name"

"I'll just tell you what I remember because memory is as close as I've gotten to building my own time machine."
Samantha Hunt – *The Invention of Everything Else*

They call Herodotus the "Father of History." In truth, Herodotus mixed history and legend into a mingled broth that while having a pleasing taste, was not all that nutritious. In other words, he was a good storyteller but he was not the best historian. The following anecdote is probably a similar mixture, a bit of Center family apocrypha if you will.

My grandfather came to the U.S. during a mass exodus from Russia in the early part of the 20th century. He arrived, like many pilgrims of that day, at Ellis Island. When my grandfather arrived, he did not understand a word of English. Imagine the general chaos that ensued when those large ships arrived at Ellis Island. In the belly of those ships were hundreds of passengers from distant lands, their hearts a jumble of hope, fear, and anxiety and their voices a cacophony of languages – all searching for safety and comfort.

Here he was, my grandfather, knowing nothing and no one. As Heinlein would say a half a century later, he was a *stranger in a strange land*. Here is what happened:

There is this large group of people in a large hall and those in charge need to process this multitude. A man in charge stands on a chair to be seen by the crowd. He yells at the top of his voice, "This group to my left, this group to my right, the rest of you stay here in the center." My grandfather is in the middle group. Recall, if you will that he speaks not a word of English. He waits his turn and finally comes to the front of the line. The person in charge calls out to him, "Name?" My grandfather says the only word he heard, the only English word he knows. He meekly replies, "Center." That name is recorded in the registry. It is in the books – really! And that, my friends, is the story of how my family got its name.

You may be wondering why this story is more apocryphal than fact. Didn't I ever ask my grandfather about the story, you ask? Nope, and that is because my grandfather was, how should I say it, a jerk of the first magnitude. He did indeed come over in the early part of the century and marry and have four children. My father was the eldest of the four. When my father was all of ten years old, my grandfather decided that the whole family thing was just not his bag and split. No forwarding address, no letters, and no child support – he just vanished into thin air. That was 1938.

Then in 1973 (that would make me 12), with a knock at my front door he was back from the dead or, in this case, Florida. I remember answering the door on that fated morning. I walked to the door and this elderly man said, "Is Sidney Center there?" I had no idea who this man was, so with great solemnity I yelled upstairs to my father, "Dad, there is old man here to see you!" And that, friends, was my introduction to my grandfather.

It would seem that he had spent the intervening decades living in Florida mostly as a fairly successful gambler. He returned because he found out he was dying and decided he wanted to connect with his children. My father did not have a burning desire to rekindle that relationship but he was kind enough to him and they reached some type of closure before my grandfather passed away.

And Speaking About Names…

It is time for a major confession. Are you sitting down? I, like thousands of others, am part of a long overlooked, feared, and generally looked down upon minority. That's right, I will admit it here in these pages: I have no middle name. There it is, out in the open. I can feel your mixture of pity and scorn. Don't tell me otherwise, I can feel it coming off you!

So how did this horrible situation occur? Well, as I am to understand it, here is how it went down back in 1961. My mother wanted to name me Brad Lee Center. You get it, right? Instead of Bradley Center, I was going to be Brad Lee Center. Say it fast and it sounds the same. My father said "no." He thought that was way too "cutesy," or at least that is how he put it. They continued to debate the whole middle name thing for a while and couldn't agree. My parents generally agreed on everything, but this was the exception. Since they couldn't decide, they concluded the best thing to do was to not give me any middle name. My father also had no middle name. He figured if it didn't impact his life in any significant way, I would be fine.

Of course, my father did not anticipate the changes in our culture and the rise of intolerance to the "middle nameless" that has arisen in the last several decades. Oh, I feel you out there, you haters. I feel you, I do. Know this, we will not continue to be oppressed and we will rise up one day and seek our just due.

Supplementary Note: When I was in my teens, I thought it would be cool to add a Z as a middle initial, simply because I thought it look good as a signature.

Signature: Brad Z. Center

I eventually grew out of that and now it is just Brad Center. Deal with it.

PART 5

And Now back to the Past

"Oh, the questions of my childhood weave a web of mystery"
Kansas, "Questions of My Childhood"

"It's not our job to try to solve the mysteries of the universe. Rather it is our job to come up with the most interesting questions."
Brad Center to Richard Kosoff, 1979

Growing up Philly

I grew up in Philadelphia in the '60s and '70s. If you are my age or thereabouts, you have seen and read things (probably on the internet) comparing those "good old days" to the world of the present and lamenting on how great our childhood was compared to today's. We look back to simpler times without smartphones, PlayStation, and intricate computer gaming. We see how addicted our kids are to these devices and know that our childhood was filled with simpler joys.

But, let's be a little honest here and admit the possibility that if we were exposed to the same gadgetry that our children are exposed to, we might act the same way our kids do. Now, don't get me wrong, I loved playing stickball, touch football, street hockey, wire-ball, Kick-the-Can, Capture the Flag and doing all the other things we did, but we did these things because there just weren't that many options available to us.

Those summer nights just "hanging out" were great, and the memories are warm and beautiful to hold. I can remember the smells, the sights, and sounds of my youth. I can touch them on quiet nights sitting on my porch in Northern Virginia. But, I wonder how selective those memories are. If I dig deep enough into those memories, mixed along with the treasure, might I find some detritus, some debris, some flotsam and jetsam, attached to these memories? Could it be that there were nights we were bored stiff, hanging around the corner with literally nothing to do? I think the answer is yes, but I, like you, probably don't want to dwell too much on those nagging little items. For now, let's misremember the past just a little bit and tell our kids how great the good old days were. They will never know.

Ahead are some stories about growing up in Philadelphia in no specific order. By the way, for those of you out there who grew up in Philly around then, why did we tie our old sneakers together and toss them over the telephone wires? I know I did it, but why?

Sneakers hanging on a wire – one of many pairs in Philadelphia

The Clown Car from Hell

I am 14 years old. My friend David wants to go to a professional lacrosse game downtown. We had (for a brief time) a professional team in Philly called the Wings. David is about 17, but he is small of stature and you would not peg him as 17 just by looking at him.

Living in Northeast Philly and getting downtown to see the Wings is a bit of an adventure. We walk a mile or so to a bus stop and take the bus to the El, officially called the Market-Frankfort Line (Who knew? Thank you, Google). From there, we take the Broad Street subway down to Spectrum Stadium. It is quite the hike. We go to the game and return to Northeast Philly just fine. We get off the bus and are just a mile from our homes, when shit goes very bad, very fast.

We get off the bus and are walking across a traffic circle called Holme Circle (reference made for all those friends and family from that area) when a car drives by. We hear a few choice curse words thrown our way, mingled just for good measure, with some very profane anti-Semitic remarks. The car is full of guys and we can smell the beer even at 35 m.p.h. David, who stands all of 5 feet 2 inches tall, decides to yell something back. A brilliant tactical move is what I am thinking. A bright neon sign lights up in my head: *We're Dead. Great, dead at the age of 14, and not much of life sampled, but at least I got to go to a fucking Wings game – oh joy!*

We pick up our pace, get across Holme Circle, and make it to the parking lot of a 7-Eleven. Suddenly, a Volkswagen Beetle pulls into the parking lot and, like a malevolent clown car, thugs of all shapes and sizes start pouring out. It is hard to say just how many of them are packed into the Volkswagen version of Stephen King's *Christine* but it looks like seven or eight of them. They don't so much get out of the car as fall out as the doors open. They are not a happy bunch of campers. That probably has something to do with whatever David had yelled back to them a few minutes ago and partly (I assume) to being jammed into that tiny, tin can of a car. They spill out of the car and split up, half jumping on me and the other half on David.

Now things get just a bit fuzzy here, but here is what I think occurred. Our lovely clown car buddies from the Volkswagen throw me down and start kicking me with gusto. This goes on for about30 seconds and they stop. Now here is the strange and kind of funny part to this tale of woe.

One guy turns to another and says, "He's got glasses on. Take his glasses off. They'll break." So, they take my glasses off my bloody face and put them on the side of the road and then proceed to go back to kicking the living shit out of me. I could not make this up. Somewhere in their warped little minds they were concerned that they would break my glasses, but it was fine to break up my face – go figure.

Let's review. . . the bus, the El, the Broad Street subway, the Wings game (who cares?), Holme Circle, anti-Semitic remark, clown car of juvenile delinquents, kicking, glasses . . . everyone up to speed?

So, let's pause for a second, and get inside my head. I was outnumbered, they were viciously kicking me, and they were bigger and stronger than I was. What is the smart play here? Lay in a fetal position until the beating stops, right? If only I were that smart. What did I do? I tried to get up and fight – continuously. I looked up and saw the main bad dude's face (there is always one main bad dude, it's a law). He was smiling down at me every time I tried to get up. That smile has found a dark and nasty place to hide in my mind, and it has kept residence there ever since. It comes out of hiding every once and awhile like an unwelcome visitor to haunt me. Some things you get to keep throughout your life whether you like them or not.

Back to the action . . . I get in one or two punches, but this only makes them angrier and prolongs the whole gosh darn party. Fortunately, after a few minutes of this fun, a truck pulls into the 7-Eleven, and the driver gets out of his rig and scares the gang off with a tire-iron. He doesn't hit them, but they jump back into their Evil Jester mobile and ride off to hell.

David and I are battered and bruised, but all things considered, we are still able to wobble on home. I enter my house, and my dad takes one look at me walking in the door and goes pale (I could have auditioned for a role in "Night of the Living Dead.")" I relay the tale to him. Does he call the police? Yes, he does, but not right away. First, he packs me in the car and off we go to scene of the crime. I think he wants a piece of those assholes, and I think he wants me to see him do it, although I am not sure he is thinking very clearly. We arrive at the 7-Eleven, but thankfully they are long gone and my dad is left standing in the parking lot with his tire-iron in his hand. Tire-irons are apparently the weapon of choice in Philly.

That is the heart of the story. We went all the way downtown and ended up getting "jumped" in our own neighborhood. Got to love that. I admit to being scared of my own shadow for a month or so afterward, and then it dawned on me. The likelihood of ever getting beat up worse was slim and I had survived. That incident colored my psychological makeup. From that point onward, I was not afraid to get into a fight because I knew that, even if I lost it would never hurt as much as that beating, and I had survived. Admittedly, this is probably not the lesson Gandhi would have learned but what the hell, he didn't grow up in Philly.

Someone Save My Life Tonight – And No, it Was Not Elton John

I'm 8 or 9, it is hard to say for sure. Living in Philadelphia and being from a middle-class family, a typical holiday is going down the shore. For those of you not from this area, that generally means the nearby Jersey Shore. If you are from Philly, you always say that you are "going down the shore." It doesn't matter whether you are going north, south, or east to get to the beach, the expression is always the same; you're always going "down," and you're always going to "the shore."

We are in Atlantic City at some hotel. It is a cloudy day and my father accompanies my brother and I to the hotel pool. It is an indoor pool which is a novelty for us. The pool is sparsely populated, so my brother and I take turns jumping off the diving board into the deep end. My father is watching from the side of the pool, fully clothed (shorts, button down shirt, black socks, sandals – you get the picture). Sidney Center, my dad, is not the epitome of style and fashion. Sidney does his own thing.

I am at the diving board, and I do the traditional cannonball into the deep end. I land and for some reason I open my mouth underwater and swallow too much water. I panic, I cannot breathe. I struggle, I flail. I break the surface, catch a glimpse of the scene and go under again. I see my father starting to rise out of his chair. I also see my brother turn from the ladder while getting out of the pool. *They are not going to get to me in time!* I again try to struggle to the surface, but I am not going to make it. Then, out of nowhere, an arm reaches me and pulls me up and out of the water. It is not my dad or brother, but rather a young kid, maybe 15 or so. He is an African American kid – strong and fast – and he is saving my life. That is about all my brain comprehends at the time. He saves me. It is just that simple. I don't know where he came from, and I don't how he got to me, but he saves me.

He pulls me to the side, where my dad and my brother help him get me out of the pool. I spit up water and breathe. I am exhausted, confused, and full of adrenaline. My dad thanks the young man. I say nothing. I am too overwhelmed to even acknowledge what is going on.

There is not much more to say, other than I owe my life to some mysterious young man vacationing in Atlantic City who acted without thinking and was there for a total stranger. Looking back on it now, I realize that I didn't even thank him. I never got his name. I know nothing about him except that he saved my life. If you are out there my friend, thank you! I owe you my life and can never repay you.

David Alan Center

I am 11 years old and my brother is 13. He goes off to New Orleans with his fraternity for a short trip. The trip didn't last more than four or five days, but its impact was going to last a very long time.

In talking about my brother, David, I am reminded of a funny scene from the TV show *Taxi*. Jim Ignatowski, the drug-ravaged space cadet/ taxi driver, is at college and is, at that point, a clean-cut guy. His face is composed, his speech eloquent, and then he takes a bite of a pot-laced brownie. His face immediately sags; his eyes start to wander and his speech becomes garbled. If you've never seen it, go to YouTube and check it out. (By the way, Tom Hanks plays one of the college students who tries to persuade Jim to take his first pot brownie – a very funny scene.)

And now back to my brother, David. So, David left for New Orleans an innocent kid and came back as a young Jim Ignatowski! What exactly happened there? I will never know, but my brother came back from the Big Easy with a big smile on his face.

Let's flash forward a few years. Can you guess my brother's favorite band during his teenage years? Would the Grateful Dead surprise you? Drugs and the Grateful Dead go together like Baskin and Robbins, like Boardwalk and Park Place, like Tutti and Frutti, or more apropos, like Cheech and Chong. I remember he kept a pegboard on his bedroom wall, composed of all his Grateful Dead concert tickets. By the time he reached 21 years old, I would estimate he had seen the Dead close to 75 times. That is a lot of travel, music, and pot for any teenager.

There is a bit of a downside here, folks. He had some great times, but the history books will record he also had five or six car crashes, some troubles in high school (it seems they actually wanted him to attend class – picky weren't they?) and several turbulent battles with my parents. On the other hand, I am not sure you survive flipping a 1972 Toyota Corolla over three times and end up with just a few scratches unless you are as high as a kite.

Yes, I know, he probably wouldn't have gotten into the accident if he were sober, but hey, I am trying to look on the bright side here.

Unlike Jim Ignatowski, my brother's story went a different and better direction. From a youth that was a bit wild and certainly filled with its share of drugs, he turned things around quite nicely. He was a respected adult and professional, a truly loving father, and beloved by his friends and family. My brother had the biggest heart imaginable and no one was more loved than he was. And yes, he still smoked a joint occasionally. I said he turned his life around. I didn't say he was a saint.

You will obviously note the past tense here. I lost my brother in 2010, and life has not been the same since. For now, put on a Grateful Dead song (any song will do, although I am partial to Uncle John's Band), relax, and chill.

P.S. To all my brother's friends (Jerry, Scott, Joel, Alan etc.), play a whole fucking album and smoke a joint because I know you will anyway.

Dave at Camp Saginaw.

Dave during high school years.

Monopoly My Way

Board games were big in the 1970s. There were significantly fewer entertainment options back then and, if it was raining outside there wasn't much else to do. I liked them all, from Trouble to Life but the big boy was Monopoly. Our games could last for days. However, over time even Monopoly lost some of its charm. So, one day, my friend David and I (he from the ill-fated Clown Car from Hell™ incident) decided to come up with our own version of the game. It took us about two or three days, but by the time we were done, we had a new version. In our new version, you bought countries as opposed to properties in Atlantic City. For example, the green properties (Pacific Ave., North Carolina Ave., and Pennsylvania Ave) became countries in the Far East (Japan, South Korea, and China). The red properties (Kentucky Ave., Indiana Ave., and Illinois Ave.) were island nations of the Caribbean. You get the gist. And of course, Park Place and Boardwalk were the U.S.S.R. and the U.S., respectively. Instead of railroads, you could buy airlines. We even wrote up individualized Chance and Community Chest cards. For a nine-year-old and a 12-year-old, it was freaking brilliant. What did we do with this great idea? Absolutely nothing. We played the game for year or so and probably threw it out. OK, so maybe we weren't exactly brilliant.

Send Lawyers Guns and Money

I am 11, and we live on Chase Road in Philadelphia. Down the street lives a good friend of my brother's, Bobby. Bobby owns a BB gun. Now, at this juncture, you are probably thinking this story is going to end badly, and, of course, you would be right, but not quite the way you might imagine.

So, my brother and I go over one day to shoot the gun in Bobby's backyard. I should state right now that I had never shot a gun before this, and knew only two things about guns: 1) jack and 2) shit. So, this is totally virgin territory for me and, like any virgin, I am nervous. Bobby and David go first and hit some targets, and then Bobby hands me the rifle and encourages me to take a few shots. I line up the rifle and pull the trigger. Actually, to be more accurate, I should say I try to pull the trigger, but nothing happens. As far as I could tell the damn thing will not pull. David and Bobby steal a quick sideways glance, but I am a little panicky right now and so I don't really process that information and its significance.

Bobby says, "What's wrong Brad? Aren't you going to take a shot?"

I am too embarrassed to tell him that I literally don't have the strength to pull the trigger, so I make-up some lame ass excuse that I am having trouble aiming it. Bobby grabs the gun and proceeds to fire off a few rounds, nailing the targets in the backyard, and hands it back to me.

He says, "Aims fine for me."

I take the gun and, again, I can't pull the damn trigger. I put the gun down and mumble, "I'll pass."

Bobby picks the gun up, smiles to my brother and says, "Works better if you release the safety."

They both crack up laughing. I turn red and mumble something about having trouble aiming it, secretly wishing I was someplace, anyplace else.

Why do some of my most vivid memories involve me getting embarrassed?

Friendship versus Facebook

At age five, it was off to kindergarten. I have a few rather insubstantial memories of kindergarten. I remember warm milk at snack time. I remember recess and finger painting on huge butcher block paper. I even vaguely recall the image of my kindergarten teacher, Mrs. Gross.

I remember these, like holding a faded picture to the light. They are flimsily held in mind like so much cotton candy at a summer fair. However, kindergarten was also memorable for another reason. It was where I met my oldest friend, Richard Kosoff. I don't have to try to remember Richard because he is (50 years later) still an integral part of my life. Still great friends after 50 years – how does that even happen? Well, I will attempt to answer that question. You work at it, like anything that matters.

We have seen and done a million different things together, from the simplest stuff when we were kids to making the time to keep the friendship alive and well as adults. When I speak of friendship, to me it means a bond that you form and a commitment you make. It is not a button you select on Facebook to someone you don't know that well or knew a dozen years ago (and yes, I realize I am ranting a bit). In my mind, Facebook has devalued the concept of friendship. Don't get me wrong, I have a Facebook account and use it as a mechanism to stay in touch with some people. But to me, true friends are few and far between, and I like it that way.

Let me tell you a tale of friendship that involves Rich and two other good friends, Jeff Jasnoff and Michael Bratman.

I was 48, and my brother had just passed away from a two-year battle with cancer. The sorrow was all encompassing. I called Richard to let him know, and we talked and reminisced about my brother for a few minutes. There wasn't much more to say during those difficult calls. Then it was off to the next call and all the other arrangements that needed to be made. I had pretty much the whole funeral to plan with the help of my brother's ex-wife Regina. Regina was a great help, but there was a ton to do and I had to think about the eulogy to boot. Because Rich lived in Los Angeles and we were in the Philadelphia area, I did not expect to see him at the funeral.

The day of the funeral arrived and I turned around and there stood Rich, Jeff, and Michael. I never asked them to come. They came from different parts of the country and they were just there, period. This is what friendship is – being there for your friend regardless if you specifically ask. It means dropping whatever you are doing to be by their side because they are in need. So, if someone asks you what friendship is, that is the answer. It is not "liking" some inane post on Facebook. It is putting your ass on the line for someone because you care.

A short side note regarding my brother's funeral. First, let me say, the service was a testament to how many people truly cared for my brother. The funeral home was packed. I stood up to give the eulogy and didn't realize how many people were jammed into that room until I turned to face the audience. It was a testament to how many lives he touched.

Now a secondary note, and this is actually a funny part of this story. At some point before the actual service began, the rabbi asked the congregation to leave the main area to give a chance for the immediate family to say goodbye. Well it seems that Richard, Jeff, and Michael did not hear the rabbi clearly, so they moved down and sat down in the third or fourth row, right behind the immediate family. The rabbi walked over to them and asked them if they would like to move closer, assuming they too were part of the immediate family. Rich, Jeff, and Mike now saw that they screwed up and should have left the room. They were embarrassed but didn't know what to do. They told the rabbi, "No we are fine where we are." Their faces said it all: *Move on Rabbi, there is nothing to see here, just move on, please!* The private goodbyes were completed and the service went beautifully. After the service, I saw the guys outside and we burst out laughing. I thought it was the funniest thing. They were stuck in "no man's" land and did not want to call attention to themselves after making the initial goof. It was painfully funny and I needed a good laugh that day.

The gang: Rich, me, Jeff and Mike on a golf trip in 2006.

And this Little Piggy. . .

For those of you who are a tad squeamish, you might want to skip ahead to the next story. You have been warned. By the way, this is a long one, so find a nice comfortable spot, relax and get yourself an alcoholic beverage of some type – you may need it.

I am 10 years old and I'm in the fourth grade at Pollock School in Philadelphia. My teacher, a kindly woman named Mrs. Thus, asks me and two other boys to roll a piano from her classroom to another class down the hallway. The piano was on wheels and rolled easily on the school's hard floors, so the job was not strenuous. Two of my classmates push the piano from behind and I steer it to the next room. I pause our progress to survey the classroom before giving the other guys the go-ahead to take the piano to the back of the classroom.

Along the near side of the classroom is a pathway between the last column of desks and the wall. Down the near side, the wall stops after about 10 feet. In the remaining length of the classroom, the classroom wall indents a few feet to allow room for the kids to hang up their coats on a large array of hooks. Halfway down the length of the room stands a pole that equally divides the room into two. I point down the nearside of the room as the best pathway to get the piano to the back of the room, and away we go.

As we start moving down the path, the piano begins to drift toward the coat hook area. I start to pull the piano back on course and this is when the pole interjects itself into the events of the morning and says, "Excuse me, I am not moving." And guess what? The pole is right, the pole isn't moving. The edge of the piano however, is in fact moving, causing the piano and pole to meet with great force. Unfortunately, the little pinky on my right hand is in the way.

There is bang, and then there is immense, white hot, blinding pain. I reach out and toss the piano aside with my left hand (it is true that you gain tremendous strength when your adrenaline is pumping.) The pain is gargantuan. If it were an animal, we are talking blue-whale-sized pain. I look down at my hand. I see blood. I see bone. I scream. I am 10. What are you expecting me to do, rip off my shirt like some movie hero and apply a tourniquet?

The teacher in the room at the time had been watching us quietly at her desk. She now jumps up and runs to my assistance, ushering me quickly to the nurse's office. We get there and of course the nurse is not there that day. The joke around school was that no matter the reason you came to the nurse's office, the first question out of her mouth would always be the same: "Did you have a good breakfast?"

"Yes, I did. Now can stop my hand from gushing blood!"

As it turns out, the gym teacher is in the office and he is cool and calm and wraps my hand up pretty good to stem the bleeding. The principal, gym teacher, and assorted staff are assembled and looking quite freaked out. They call my mom and she gets a taxi over to the school in short order. My mom does not drive and so a taxi is the mode of transportation for the day. We get into the taxi and have him take us to my neighborhood doctor just a mile down the road. I should state, at this point, that the pain has not gone anywhere. It is a throbbing like a bass drum, reverberating through my entire body.

At the doctor's, we are rushed into his office. He opens the wrapping and his eyes go wide. He says, and I quote, "Oh God, I can't touch this. Get him to the hospital now!"

I am very reassured now – right? No panic in my mind at all. Shit! Shit! Shit!

Off to the hospital we go. That is another 20-minute ride. In the taxi are me, my mom, the taxi driver (who is a little frazzled) and my new best friend, Mr. Pain. Mr. Pain couldn't bear to leave me now, not after becoming so close, so fast. We are buddies.

We get to the emergency room and they immediately operate. My finger is broken in two places, the artery is smashed, and my tendon is shredded like so much pulled pork. The operation takes two hours or so, I am not entirely sure – time is fluid at this point. The operation is finished and I fall asleep as they wheel me up to the room.

I wake up to find my hand wrapped and my finger in a splint. My finger is a lovely shade of purple. And just to make the day complete, my buddy Mr. Pain is there in the room with me. My mom is there as well, but Mr. Pain has all my attention at the moment. My mom asks how I am. I tell her about good old Mr. Pain and she gets the nurse to give me some relief.

The good news for me is that I am at Rolling Hill Hospital and both my aunts work there as managers on the administrative side of the house, so I am treated like a prince. My finger takes a long time to heal but with the loss of the tendon, my little pinky is no longer straight, rather it is curled, like a cheese doodle. I can make a fist, but I cannot straighten it out.

Post Script: About a month later, I had to get the stitches out. History will note that my mom was a rock through the whole accident. She got me to the hospital, sat with me all night in the hospital, and was everything you would want your mother to be in such a situation. But now I must get the stitches out. Turns out my mom was a rock because she had a ton of adrenaline coursing through her veins on the day of the accident. Well there is no adrenaline flowing through her on the day I get my stitches out. So, we are in the doctor's office and as the doctor begins to pull out the stitches, my mother faints dead away. They take my mom into the other room to revive her. I think the whole office is in there taking care of my mom. I am sitting there hand out on the table, completely forgotten. Ten minutes later, I am still sitting there, so I figure I had better yell for some assistance. Eventually I get someone's attention and they finish taking the stitches out. My mom: great in a medical emergency, not so good with the common everyday doctor visits.

Paregoric

Does anyone remember Paregoric? When we were kids, my parents would give my brother and me this horrid tasting stuff for various ailments. It had to be the foulest tasting stuff man has ever created. Take some week-old eggs, mix them generously with some castor oil, then add some haggis, some pickled beets, some sauerkraut, and maybe just a touch of vinegar. That gives you some sense as to how horrible this stuff tasted. My brother and I would turn white as a sheet at the mere mention of the word.

Why would my loving and kind parents give this stuff to us? Well it was kind of a cure-all back in the '60s. So, I did a little investigating and here is what I found:

- Paregoric was a household remedy to control diarrhea in adults and children; as an expectorant and cough medicine, to calm fretful children; and to rub on the gums to counteract the pain from teething.
- The principal active ingredient in Paregoric is powdered opium.
- The formula for Paregoric, includes opium, anise oil, benzoic acid, camphor, glycerin, alcohol, purified water, and just for good measure – anhydrous morphine.
- Until 1970, Paregoric could be purchased in the United States at a pharmacy without a medical prescription.

Well, isn't that interesting? I got morphine and opium as a kid. Let's hear it for loose government regulation of controlled substances. I can't blame my parents. I bet they had no idea what was in this stuff. But wow!

Valentine's Day Mystery

I am six and in first grade. It's February 13th and our teacher tells us to bring in Valentine's cards for the class. I set to work and put together a list for my mom of all my classmates. I diligently sign my name on each card, but something is bothering me. I am not sure what it is, but something is not right. I think I have forgotten someone. I am 6 and I am already suffering memory loss issues! I think and think, but I cannot remember who I am missing. I am beginning to obsess about it and my mother tries to calm me down. She says not to worry about it, it will come to me, now go to bed.

Reluctantly I go to bed, but sleep eludes me and I toss and turn. I cannot let it go. Then, suddenly, it hits me like wave of cool ocean spray in the face. I know who I forgot. I run down the stairs and scream "Debbie Picarelli! Debbie Picarelli, with the patch over her eye." I keep repeating this over and over as I run down the steps two at a time. My mom and dad just look on with amused bewilderment. I am just repeating the name and eye patch thing over and over. I am providing them no context at all.

My father wasn't in the room when we were doing the Valentines and my mother has momentarily forgotten my Valentine's Day angst from earlier in the evening, so they are understandably confused. Then my mom figures it out and explains it to my dad. They calm me down and we get Debbie Picarelli a Valentine Day card.

From that point on, if I could not remember something, it was referred to as a "Debbie Picarelli moment." I think it was the whole patch-over-the-eye thing that made it stick in my parent's memory. And, by the way, I have no idea why she had a patch over her eye.

Dogs, Rabbits, and Alligators Oh My!

As a kid, I always enjoyed taking care of animals. We had a couple of dogs but also a variety of other pets crossed our threshold as well. I took in the occasional wounded or stray rabbit, or whatever. We had goldfish and some turtles as well. At one point, we even had a fairly large box turtle which proved to be too big to take care of properly so we ended up setting him free in Pennypack Park in Northeast Philly.

When I was 10 and we lived in a small house in northeast Philly. My mother's older sister, my Aunt Evelyn (Evie for short), was vacationing in Florida. One afternoon, my mother called me into the kitchen to tell me the mail has just arrived and there is a package from my Aunt Evie all the way from Florida. I was suddenly all ears. A dozen thoughts crossed my mind and I was anticipating a nice little gift from my aunt.

My mother took the package (a small rectangular box) and laid it on the kitchen counter. She opened one end and peered inside. It was dark but she could tell there was something in there. Then all of a sudden, a small baby alligator ran out – really, a baby alligator! My mother, who was not too fond of animals to begin with and certainly not keen on anything reptilian, shrieked, jumped back and stared in disbelief. I can't say for sure exactly what I was expecting, but a baby alligator was probably not on my top ten list!

Just what the hell is going on around here," I asked myself. *Why was there a miniature dinosaur crawling on our kitchen counter?* I stared and needed a moment to process the information. Suddenly a sense of calm surrounded me and I walked over and picked up the frightened creature. He looked up at me and there was an instant bond. His eyes said, "*help me.*" From that day forward we were inseparable. I named him Alex and he was my best friend from then on. We kept him for ten years. The neighbors were freaked out, but no ever bothered me or my family. One day, the Philadelphia Zoo showed up and took him away. I continued to visit him at the zoo, and we remained close until he passed away in 1987 from unknown causes.

What a lovely story! None of that is true but I think it makes a lovely little story. Here is the true version of events that unfolded after my mother opened the box...

My mom I were both dumbfounded. Cautiously, we picked up the freaked out little thing and put him into a plastic bowl. I never got a satisfactory explanation from my aunt about why she mailed a live alligator to us. She explained (oddly) that she thought the little feller would not survive the trip. What was she thinking? Did she think I wanted a petrified, stiff, dead alligator? I had no clue what was going through her head, but now we had a live alligator on our hands. He was small and kind of cute in a reptilian sort of way. We had no clue how to feed him or take care of him. I went to the library, but I found nothing there of any real help. There was no readily available manual entitled *How to Feed and Care for Your Baby Alligator*. We gave it our best shot, but the truth was, that little guy was not exactly in his natural environment and he just would not eat. My mom even tried feeding him tuna right out of the can. One morning, he just didn't wake up. My mom was probably secretly thrilled, but she was kind enough not to say that out loud, at least not to me. We buried him in the backyard. We did not flush him down the toilet and so any myths about alligators in the sewer are not my responsibility.

Hercules

Speaking of pets, I need to mention my dog, Herc. His full name was Hercules, but he was such a scrawny, mangy little feller that calling him Hercules is akin to calling Donald Trump brilliant (sorry, Dear Reader, I really should refrain from political asides, but Trump is just such an easy target). We got him when I was about 14 or so and he was a great dog. He was a bit of an escape artist, and so while we had a fence in the back, he would dig holes under the fence and make an escape. There were a few times he was gone for a day or so, but he always managed to find his way home. I took Herc with me to Virginia when I moved there, and he was a constant companion until I was 26 years old. He got old and sick and I took him to the veterinarian, but there was not much they could do and so, in the end, I had him put to sleep. I stayed with him as they gave him the needle and watched the lights slowly leave his sad, little eyes but that is what you do. You never leave your dog with strangers – not at the end.

The Moment?

I am 12 and what is about to occur has everything to do with a short story I will not read for another 15 years. I am in the schoolyard of my elementary school – Pollock School. It is recess and we are playing a game of what my gym teacher refers to as "handball." This version is not what most people refer to as handball where you hit a small ball against a wall; this is sort of baseball with a large dark red playground ball. The game is played just like baseball except that instead of tagging or throwing someone out on a specific base, you "call them out" from the pitcher's mound. The ball is thrown to the pitcher from the field of play and the pitcher yells (for example) "First Base." If the pitcher has the ball in his hand, and the player has not reached first base yet, he is out. Additionally, instead of swinging a bat, you simply punch the ball out into the field of play. I provide all this minutia so that you can understand the following. . .

We are playing in the Pollock School handball championship. Each class has played each other during the year and now we are at the championship game. The score is tied, but time for recess is rapidly running out. I am up to bat, and I get a single to get things moving. The next two kids do the same. The bases are now loaded. I take a lead off third as the next batter steps to the plate. He hits a ball to the infield, and I take off for home. The following sequence of events unfolds in about two seconds: I cross home plate, the pitcher calls "Home" after he gets the ball from the infield (too late), and then the bell ending recess rings. We win and my teammates literally pick me up and carry me off the playground.

It is a one-of-kind moment; the kind you don't always appreciate to the fullest at the time but that you get to savor over and over in your mind. I try to soak it all in. I try to capture in my mind what I see, what I hear, and what I feel. I want to hold on to this feeling for as long as I can.

I am now 27 and have just finished a short story called "The Cheese Stands Alone." The story tells the tale of a man who stumbles into a strange bookstore. The bookstore proprietor (some type of sorceress) tells the man that whatever he seeks, the answers are here in this bookstore. He need only but look. The sorceress then tells the man that she has a book that will tell him the best moment of his life! He looks around and sees others in the bookstore, but they are all frozen in place and he is understandably concerned. He asks why they are frozen and the proprietor tells him they got the answer they were looking for and no longer need anything else. He doesn't want to be frozen in a catatonic state, but he is insatiably curious and finally asks for the book. He finds out the best moment of his life occurred when he was but a child and that nothing else in his entire life will top the pure joy of that moment so long ago. However, the protagonist does not freeze like the others in the book store but continues on, even knowing that his best moment is behind him.

I read those words, and I was dumbstruck. Could my best moment have occurred some 15 years ago? I recall the playground, my cheering classmates, the adulation and wonder – was that the highpoint of my life? I close the book. It can't be so. I refuse to let it be. With determination and hope, I move on.

Golfing with Sid

There have been hundreds of books written about golf but they all tend to boil down to these basic facts: Golf is a game of extremes; it is a game you can love and hate simultaneously.

I learned the game from my father. When and where he started playing I am not sure. I can tell you however, that he never took it seriously and never took a lesson, and both facts were on equal display whenever he was on the course.

I enjoyed every game we ever played together and so did anyone else who had the privilege to play a round of golf with my father. So, I can thank Sidney Center for my love/hate relationship with the game of golf.

My father had a certain way about him. He spoke with the utmost confidence about pretty much any subject. Sometimes he knew exactly what he was talking about, other times he was simply bullshitting you, and sometimes he thought he knew the right answer but wasn't exactly on-the-mark. But, because he was extremely well-read and knowledgeable, I didn't always know when to nod and ingest the knowledge, when to call bullshit, and when to double-check his facts. When it came to golf, my dad gave me plenty of advice and, unfortunately for me, most of it was well, just plain wrong. In the case of golf, he wasn't bullshitting me, but since he never took a lesson he just didn't have the right information to give – but he tried.

One afternoon, we were out on a local course in Philly and we came to a short par three of about 150 yards. I teed off and put it within six inches of the hole. Obviously, I was thrilled, but what I didn't know was this: that I would never get closer to a hole-in-one than I did that afternoon with my father. See what I mean about a love/hate relationship? I recall that my dad smiled at me and at my shot. He was proud, but I think he also knew what a fluke that was.

In addition to playing golf at this local course in Philly, we played a course near Ocean City, New Jersey, when I was an adult and spending vacation time there. My father passed away in 2006, and I make a special point to go back to both these courses on occasion. I can sort of feel him there when I play. I remember after my father passed away, my brother put a golf ball in my father's casket and whispered to him, "Hit 'em straight up there, Dad." Not much more to say than that.

My father having a good time at a Phillies game circa 1967.

Snow Mountain

One wintry day back in 1973, Richard and I decided to go to the movies. It had snowed heavily the night before. The snow came in big, fat, wet flakes and when it was finished, it covered everything. After the snow, the snowplows came out and started clean-up operations. The result was that Mother Nature and Philadelphia's Sanitation Department (a most unnatural coupling if ever there was one) had created a miniature mountain range with mountains as high as 15 to 20 feet tall in the parking lot behind the movie theater.

Perhaps it was the mix of wet snow with slightly colder air. Perhaps it was how the snowplows had condensed the snow into these mini mountains. Perhaps it was the added ingredient of Philadelphia smog and grit. Whatever the recipe, the mountain range that now stood behind the movie theater was perfect.

The mountains were easy to climb, and more importantly, the plows had left gigantic boulders scattered about on the makeshift mountains. The boulders were a couple of feet across but just the right consistency to enable us to pick them up and toss them at each other without causing any real harm. They contacted with a solid thud and then broke in two across your shoulder. Additionally, we could reach down and without any effort whatsoever scoop up a snowball for added ammunition. No need to smooth and pat down the snow, they were perfect just picking them up from the side of the mountain.

Rich and I spent hours on those mountains tossing boulders at each other and playing one sort of game or another. We played with abandon and, strangely enough, neither one of us got hurt for all the rough play. At some point, we both looked up and simultaneously decided to call it a day. We were exhausted. I have never experienced a more perfect snow or afternoon just having fun.

Gymnastic Brilliance

I was 13 and in gym class and so begins another slightly embarrassing tale but, truth be told, is there any other kind when we are talking teenagers and gym class? At 13, I was a pretty athletic kid. I could play just about every sport, and I had been playing basketball consistently for a few years. However, basketball, football, baseball, none of them are adequate preparation for pure gymnastics or as our gym teacher liked to call it, "the apparatus." Sounds vaguely sinister when you call it "the apparatus" in my opinion.

On this particular day, we were introduced to the still rings. We were given instructions on how to do simple stuff like an inverted hang and some mysterious move called a "Bird's Nest." The Bird's Nest requires that you hook your feet in the rings and then you kind of invert your body so that your stomach and head point to the floor. This is not a particularly difficult move, except if you get your feet stuck in the rings after completing the basic move. If that happens, then the whole thing becomes one giant clusterfuck. This, unfortunately, was my fate. I ended up hanging completely upside down for a full minute until the gym teacher mercifully got me down. I might add that the whole gym class was watching this gymnastic vaudeville act and laughing hysterically. Was I embarrassed? Hell, yes, I was embarrassed. The only good news was that I could blame my bright red face on the blood rushing to my head from hanging upside down.

Saginaw Reflections

As a kid, I went to Camp Saginaw for several summers. It was an overnight camp in Oxford, Pennsylvania. Camp Saginaw was a prestigious camp and expensive. In fact, it was too expensive for the Center Family. My parents had to work at the camp to enable us to afford to attend. My dad took an administrative job and my mom worked in the office. Heck, the first year we even brought our dog to the camp.

I have fond memories of my years at Saginaw. I was "All Around Camper" one year and "Color War Captain" one year. I should probably explain the term Color War as it sounds vaguely racist. At the end of the summer, the camp was divided up into two teams – the Red Team and the Blue Team. There are contests of all types for about a week and points are given to each team accordingly. At the end of week there is a Songfest and each team is tasked to learn and perform three songs. Yes, that's right, Color War is decided by a singing contest. This brings the teams together and reinforces teamwork and collaboration.

I remember a ton of things from camp. I can harken back to the athletic triumphs, if I wish. I can reminisce on the friendships from so long ago. I can do all of that, but what I really want to talk about is the music at Saginaw. The music was woven into the fabric of everything we did, it bound us and grounded us, and it personified a culture of teamwork, family, and honor.

There was music everywhere. We sang at Saturday morning services. We sang the blessing over bread at meals. We sang during Color War and, most importantly, when you got to be one of the older campers, you became a Hillman and the Hillman had the greatest songs. The Hillman would march into the mess hall accompanied by the theme from the movie *The Great Escape* and sing their hearts out to the Hillman marching song. This may seem an odd thing to take away from those years, but it was something that built spirit and pride. Maybe there are some lessons to be learned from Camp Saginaw that might be good for society as a whole. I'm just saying . . .

Sidney Center – Military Genius

That title might be the biggest exaggeration in this entire book. My father's military career was less than stellar. He served in World War II as a private. He never made it past private because my father possessed a couple of character traits not truly appreciated by the military: He was inquisitive and he did not like taking orders. Is it any wonder he never made it past private?

When my father was ordered to perform some specific task, he would pause and ask why. Why was it necessary to "take that hill" or to move that equipment from here to there? He wanted things to make sense. That was not the military way. Hence, my father had the opportunity to spend many fascinating hours in the brig or stockade! If you think going to the brig would change my father's attitude, think again. He would get out and keep quiet for a while only to speak up once again and then back to brig. I really think the Army had no idea what to do with him.

At some point, whether it was a mistake or based on some commander's utter frustration, they sent my dad off to Paris. He was assigned to a unit responsible for radio repair. My dad knew nothing about radios or how to repair them. The military did not care. So, he spent his days doing a little repair work, but basically he wandered the streets of Paris. Not a bad way to spend the last days of the war.

My father never participated in a great battle. He never saved the lives of his fellow soldiers. He was never decorated for bravery. He never did those things, not because he was unwilling but rather because he was simply a man who asked questions. He wanted to see things done in a logical manner and so, he never found himself on the battlefield. He was the Mr. Spock of his generation, but this was not Star Fleet and it was not the 23rd century; his logic and inquisitive mind were not well-received. My father's major military accomplishment was simply coming home in one piece to start a family, becoming a teacher and administrator and to raise his family with dignity and honor. Not a bad way to spend your life – all things considered.

My father during his illustrious military career.

Big Mitz in the Lime Light

I love the theater, and my wife and I try to attend a few plays each year at Washington D.C.'s Arena Stage. Recently, we went to see a reproduction of "Little Foxes" by Lillian Hellman. We enjoyed the show and a few weeks later ended up in Philadelphia visiting my mom and mentioned that we had just seen that play. She smiled and said that she had starred in that very same play back when she was a young woman in her local community theater group. The play revolves around a manipulative character by the name of Regina. My mother played Regina, and while she is totally unlike Regina in real life, she relished the chance to play such a character.

I knew my mother had acted as a young woman. The family photo albums contain a myriad of photos of her time on the stage, but it was still an interesting coincidence to know she starred in a play we had just seen. My mom got the acting bug when she was young. She did some local radio shows and eventually migrated to local community theater. She appeared in several plays in the Philadelphia area. She was quite good and could memorize not only her lines but pretty much the entire script if need be. Personally, I have no idea how she could memorize all those lines. That talent is beyond my grasp. It was kind of her superpower. I can easily get up in front of a large crowd and talk or even give a speech, but memorizing all those lines? Forget it.

I remember a story she told me once about a play she was in back in the day. That play took place over 50 years ago, but my mom's memory was as clear as if she had been on stage the day before. My mom told me that her co-star was a bit of a drinker and must not have cared too deeply for the play or he cared more about his drinking habit because, one afternoon he came to the stage completely hammered. He could barely stand, let alone remember all his lines. As I said, my mom had a great memory, so she is literally on stage holding this chump up and feeding him his lines and hoping he will sober up as the play continues. She did her best, but that afternoon's matinee showing did not go down in theater history. To add to the total embarrassment, he kept having to go to the bathroom and would miss his entrances. It was (only in hindsight) quite comical. Unfortunately, the play was not a comedy, or at least it was not intentionally a comedy.

Ultimately, the stage was not where my mom would make her mark because at some point, she met a guy named Sidney Center. Not that my father forced her to choose between the stage and marriage, but rather my mother never had the intense drive to make this her career. She loved Sidney Center more than anything else. The theater provided her with some great memories but ultimately it was not her life calling.

A picture of my mom's stage days.

Parenting

Throughout my life, I have heard friends and acquaintances alike tell me some rather disturbing stories of their childhood. These stories deal with parents who ignore their children, treat them as possessions, or who create such a dysfunctional home environment that their children are starved for consistency and belonging.

If I had such stories, I am sure I would also feel the need to fill this book with those accounts and thereby cleanse myself of the anger and resentment from a troubled childhood. But fortune smiled upon me, and I have no such stories. I did not starve for affection. I was never hurt physically or emotionally. I had good parents, and while no one is perfect, they created a good home and a loving family atmosphere. Therefore, in this book, there are no horror stories from my youth. Instead I offer a simple thank you to both my father and mother for all their care and love.

I would add one more thing. I think I was darn lucky in the gene pool lottery. From my mother, I received just the right amount of ambition, the ability to speak comfortably in front of any audience, and my warped sense of humor. From my father, I got an inquisitive mind and love of learning. Not bad, except I also got his bad eyesight and a receding hairline. All things considered, I made out okay.

PART 6

High School and Other Reflections

"We are our own dragons as well as our own heroes, and we have to rescue ourselves from ourselves"
Tom Robbins, *Still Life with Woodpecker*

Leaning into a Left Hook

I am 17 and Rich Kosoff and I are in my car heading home from a local pizza joint called Aldo's. It's snowing and the roads are a mess. As we make a turn from one side street onto another, my car begins to skid out from beneath me. We are in the process of the turn and the front half of the car wants to go forward and the back half wants to fade to the right. My keen mind determines that this is not a good situation.

Pointing to a parked car on the right side of the road just past the intersection, Rich says, "We are not going to make it."

"We'll make it," I say.

"Turn in the direction of the skid!" he yells, putting his hands on the dashboard and bracing for impact.

Fuck that, I think. I am turning in the opposite direction and slamming on the brakes. Intellectually, I know that turning in the direction of the skid is the right thing but as the comedian once said, that's like leaning into a left hook. I pump the brakes harder.

"We are not going to fucking make it!" Rich yells. His scream is deafening. The car on the side of the road grows larger every second. We continue to slide in slow motion towards the parked car.

"We're going to make it!" I scream back.

The car finally stops – one inch before the parked car. I start to breathe again. Rich unclenches every muscle in his body and exhales.

I turn to Rich. "Told you," I say.

Rich laughs a nervous laugh. "Obviously, it was a piece of cake."

We have to get out of the car and push it back a few feet so I can complete the turn but really, easy as pie.

Working for Rich's Dad (Big F...king Al)

I am 16 and many of my friends have gone off to summer camp to work as counselors, but I decide to stay home for the summer; however, I need to earn some extra cash, and if I am not going to work as a counselor I need to do something. So, I decide to go work for Rich's dad who we affectionately called Big Al.

I think I need to describe Big Al for just a moment. To be brutally honest, I referred to him as Big Fucking Al. That was his persona, and the name fit. I didn't actually call him that name to his face, mind you. I was not a complete idiot. For, you see, Al was a tall, strong, barrel-chested man, and he was the kind of guy who would tell you if you were being a dumb-ass straight to your face. In fact, I know he used that exact phrase at me on several occasions. Don't be put off. I was a teenager and sometimes I acted like, well, a dumb-ass. I liked Al, but it was not like I could relax around him. I needed to be on my toes and pay attention. I was always trying to avoid a possible "dumb-ass" comment.

Big Al was in the construction business. I don't think, given my description of Al, that this should come as a surprise. If God was going to mold an image of a general contractor, he would start with Al.

It's summer, and I am working for Al on several construction sites that he is managing. Let it be said straight off, that I have no handyman type skills. That may be an overstatement. If it can be said to have negative skills, that would be a more accurate description of my overall capabilities. What I have is brute strength and that is how Al used me.

As I said, it is summer and I am busting my butt for Al on this one particular job. One day on the site, Al asks me to lay down some insulation in the house we had just about completed. I nod. *Sure, no problem*, I think to myself. How hard could that be? Besides, it will get me out of the sun. Each and every experience working for Al is basically a new one for me. I had never put down insulation before, and I am sure Al knew that.

Al shows me the insulation and says to get to work. Not much more than that. So, off I go. I roll out the pink stuff all through the attic of the house. No problem, except that about half-way through, I start to itch all over my hands and arms. I figure I must be allergic to fiberglass. I finish up because I am not about to walk over to Big Al to complain and wimp out simply because I itch. I get out of the attic and walk outside, and then I get a good look at my arms. It's like I have a thousand tiny cuts all over my arms.

I glance over and see Al over by his truck. He is laughing and smirking all at the same time, which is an interesting look to hold. He knows what's happened. In fact, I am quite sure, *he knew what would happen*! I look at him bewildered. Al looks up at me.

He says, "What did you just do?"

I say, "I just put down the insulation you asked me to."

"And what is the insulation made of, dumb-ass?" He says this laughingly. I told you that phrase and I got to be close friends.

"Fiberglass," I say.

"Yes, the key word there is 'glass.' Those are cuts from the fiberglass. You should have worn long sleeves and gloves."

I nod, but in my head, I am thinking, *Yep, good information. Good tip to save until I am done the job. That would have been a nice little piece of information to share before I started!* But that was what it was like to work for Big Al. You learned things – sometimes the hard way. He was teaching me a lesson, and it was a lesson I wasn't going to forget. Ask questions before you start a job, dumb-ass.

Fractions of an Inch – At Least that was the Plan

I am 16, and I stand about six feet, four inches tall and weigh about 185 pounds. It's summertime and a few of us are hanging around one night outside my home on Kent Lane, not doing much, just hanging out. Rich is there and so is our friend Steve Pollack.

I turn to Rich and more specifically to Steve, and say, "Steve, I've been working on my jab and my hook. I bet I can throw a punch and come within fractions of an inch from hitting you. Trust me, I'm not actually going to hit you."

Steve says, "Fine go ahead."

Steve is a nice guy, but way too trusting. I tell Steve to stand very still, and I throw a beautiful overhand right directly at his chin and, what the hell, I hit him. The punch is at about half strength but even so, it was a solid shot. Steve just stands there. He is dazed and confused but still standing. He stays that way for a minute or so, collecting himself. He rubs his chin and says, very softly, "Fractions of an inch?"

I am stunned as well but for obviously different reasons. "Steve" I say, "Are you OK? I am really, really sorry. I guess I miscalculated."

This is the understatement of the year. He says he is fine, well, sort of fine. He looks like he just woke up from a very weird dream, but still isn't sure if he is awake or not.

Looking back on it, I am not quite sure I would have reacted that nicely. I think I would have insisted on a little *quid pro quo*. So, once again Steve, sorry about that. I am sure that, next time, I will get it right. Trust me, I've been practicing – really.

Addendum 2017: I just saw Steve Pollack after many years. It turns out he doesn't even remember the infamous "fractions-of-an-inch" incident. Rich and I recall it quite vividly, perhaps the punch resulted in some strange memory loss situation or perhaps my punch was just not that memorable.

Icarus – "Borne on the Wings of Steel" (Kansas 1975)

I am 18, and I want nothing more than to have my own car. My dad and I talk it over and he agrees. I was going to Temple University in downtown Philadelphia and I needed a way to get up and back to school.

I knew I was not getting some expensive car, but I secretly hoped for something, anything that was even remotely cool. I had nightmares of driving to school in an AMC Pacer, or worse, a AMC Gremlin.

On a nice autumn weekend afternoon, my dad took me down to a used car dealership and we looked around. I scanned the lot. There were some sad cars out there and I started to think my nightmares were going to come true. I recall looking deep into the lot searching for something that approximated "coolness." I turned my head slowly, looking, searching, and my eyes finally landed on a 1972 Dodge Charger. It was blue with a black vinyl top, and I was instantly and forever in love.

I turned to my father with a longing and wistful look. I was afraid he would take one look at that car and tell me to forget it. He looked it over, had a conversation with the salesman and told me it was mine. I could not fucking believe it! I mean, seriously, the car was cool and my dad was all in. Six hundred dollars later the car was all mine.

I named the car Icarus after the Greek myth and Kansas song mentioned above. Now, the car was great, but Icarus was a bit finicky (and, yes, I realize I am anthropomorphizing here, but this car deserved it). While he was fast and strong, he was a tad injury prone. Icarus was a high-performance car and a lot of the parts were specialty items, so repairs (and there were a few) ended up costing a pretty penny.

We took the car to New York on a trip once and I believe we hit 110 m.p.h. on the freeway. Icarus loved it – he cruised, no issues. I realize how stupid it was going 110 m.p.h., but they say that your brain is not fully formed at 20 years old, and I am fine using that as my excuse now.

In addition to side trips, I drove the car to Temple University almost every day and loved every minute in that car. But, something about that car attracted thieves. I had three car batteries stolen out of the car at Temple!

What I didn't know was that when I named the car "Icarus," I was tempting fate and providing some unwelcome foreshadowing. One summer day, I noticed a slight leak coming from the fuel line as it entered the carburetor (or at least that is my general memory of the problem). As I said repairs could be expensive with Icarus, so to save a few bucks I attempted to fix it myself. That was a huge mistake!

A week later, I went downtown to Temple to visit my dear friend Valerie (who later turned out to be my wife Valerie but that is another story), when smoke started billowing into the front seat from the vents. The engine was on fire! I pulled off to the side of the road about a mile from my home, jumped out of the car, and dove to a grassy area adjacent to the sidewalk. I looked up and waited for the subsequent explosion to occur. I waited – no explosion. I had been raised on '70s TV shows, and cars always blew up when they caught fire. It was the law. Icarus did not blow up. The gas tank was nowhere near the engine, and so Icarus, somewhat like his mythical namesake, slowly burned. As I said, I did make a dramatic dive to the ground, and I am sure it looked very impressive, but there were no explosions.

Eventually, a passing car stopped, and the guy offered me a ride up the street to a nearby fire station. By the time we arrived, the firemen told me that they had already received a call and a fire truck was probably already there. The guy drove me back and I saw poor Icarus on the side of the road, with fireman dousing him with water. He looked so sad.

I walked on home. There was nothing else to do. I looked and felt horrible. I was black with smoke on the outside and totally disheartened on the inside. I loved that car! I loved the way I felt driving it. I loved the way I looked driving it. Icarus helped turn a somewhat awkward teenager into and something approximating "cool."

My parents took one look at me and their mouths opened in alarm. I quickly gave them a summary of what had happened. Not much they could do either. The next day we had Icarus towed to our mechanic and he said the engine was molten slag! He gave us $100 for the tires. I was crushed. I have owned any number of cars since then, but that was the only car that I truly loved.

Basketball 101

Basketball Story #1

The first rule of basketball is: You do not talk about basketball. Oops, sorry that's *Fight Club* and a totally different story. The first rule of basketball is to score on your side of the court. A rule that should be followed, as I will explain.

I am 11 and I play for a local team in my area of Philadelphia. I am the tallest one on the team and so, as my name would dictate, I play center for the team. It is Saturday afternoon and we are playing another local team and we are beating them soundly. We are a pretty good team.

We come out of the locker room after half-time, and we jump ball at half-court. As the center, I do the honors. The referee tosses the ball up, and I tap the ball towards a teammate, but he fumbles it and the ball is loose on the floor and everyone is trying to get hold of it. It's like the referees put Vaseline on the ball during half-time because no one seems to be able to get ahold of the ball. Finally, the ball squirts out and I grab it. I turn and head down the court towards the basket. I can hear the crowd cheering or yelling, it is hard to tell, and I make a perfect lay-up into the basket. I turn and two of my teammates are yelling and laughing at the same time. I made a perfect lay-up in the wrong basket. I turn red. I am not sure what to say or do – the situation is too weird to know how to act. I smile and hand the ball to the referee. We are up twenty points, so as the saying goes – no harm, no foul. I thankfully score a few more times during the game and we win by around a dozen points. Whew!

Now, I must say that, in my defense, we had just come back from half-time and had switched sides. Also the ball, as I said, was flopping around the court like a fish out of water before I picked up and took off for the basket. Perhaps that is not a great defense, but it is all I have.

Basketball Story #2

When I was about 16 or so, I could finally dunk a basketball. For about two or three years, dunking a basketball was just about my favorite thing, period. Dunking a basketball is a complete and total adrenaline rush. It is as powerful an act you can do without hurting anyone. You are up above the rim, and there is a brief moment where everything seems to pause, it is the briefest of instants, and you jam the ball down with all the force you can muster. It is an addictive power rush, and I would do it until my knees ached from the pounding and my wrist was bruised from slamming it against the rim. The unabashed truth is this: Dunking a basketball is like having an orgasm, except that you can pretty much do it nonstop.

At about this time, my mother (who was working for the Philadelphia Housing Authority) got a request from her boss to help him with a commercial they were doing for Mayor Frank Rizzo. This will take a minute to explain but essentially, Rizzo wanted to run for re-election but was prohibited because the Philadelphia Charter prevented him from running for a third term. Rizzo wanted the charter changed to allow him to run and he was running ads on TV to get the Philadelphia Charter changed.

Trust me, there is a basketball story in here soon. The TV crew has an idea: Let's get two young kids on camera to talk about the Charter change. The idea was to garner the younger vote for the charter change. The question was, what type of setting or "hook" could they use in the commercial to make it memorable and effective. They decided that two young kids playing basketball would be perfect. My mother's boss offered up me and my brother. My brother Dave was two years older than I was and of voting age, hence he got the speaking part in the TV ad. I would not classify my brother or myself as big Rizzo fans, probably the opposite, but this was less about if we liked Rizzo and more about changing the charter; besides it was chance to be on TV.

Here is how it played out. David and I were put on a basketball court in some playground in South Philly and David was told to say something like,

"I am not sure if I am a Frank Rizzo fan, but shouldn't we get a chance to vote for who we want? Let's change the charter and give everyone a chance to decide for themselves. Vote Yes for the charter change!"

For my part, I was standing in the background as my brother said these lines. He then paused and passed me the ball and I dunked it into the basket. Sounds simple, and I guess it was, but we ended up doing at least 30 or so takes of this one scene. I kept looking over at Dave. He had flubbed his lines a few times, but mostly he was getting it right. The camera crew kept saying, "Let's try another take, we want to make sure we have a really good one." By the time we were done, I was all dunked out.

The commercial aired about a dozen times or so and my brother and I basked in the limelight for a few weeks. I wish to God we had a video tape of it, but sadly this great cinematic masterpiece is lost to the world. I would love to see my brother again, if only on video.

Basketball Story #3

A year or so later, I was playing on the George Washington High School varsity basketball team. I will cut to the chase. We sucked, to put it mildly. I don't think we won a game all year. I was basically "ok," that is really the best I can say about my personal play. I would love to go back and tell the 17-year-old version of Brad to relax and be more confident. One of the things you hear from sports broadcasters is that, as you get comfortable on the court, the game slows down for you. I just never got there. I still had good time and had some good moments here and there. But I would love to go back in time and place my adult mind inside my 17-year-old body. It would probably do wonders for my game. I had some physical talent, but I lacked the mental and emotional maturity needed to excel.

During my playing days at George Washington High School, the *Philadelphia Bulletin* (which was one of the two papers in the Philadelphia market back then) did a sports quiz one week. This was not a regular fixture in the paper, and come to find out, I was a question in the quiz. The question was: *Name the only public high school basketball player whose name is the same as his position?* I was a celebrity for the week. It didn't improve my play on the court, but it was pretty cool regardless. I guess I should thank my departed grandfather for not speaking any English when he got off the boat!

Basketball Story #4

After high school, I would still play ball now and then just for fun. I was at a nearby playground in a pick-up game one afternoon having a good time, when things went decidedly south in just a few seconds. I wish that we had a movie soundtrack for our lives. In the movies, when something bad is about to happen the music will give you some clue as to what awaits you in the next scene. Not so in the real world. Not at all. So, because I had no soundtrack, I had no idea about the painful events that were about to unfold. Here's what happened.

I was heading back on defense when the other team stole the ball from our point guard and headed down for an easy lay-up. I was close behind and determined to block the shot from behind. Unfortunately, the guy who had stolen the ball was left-handed and, when he went up for the lay-up, his right elbow flailed backwards, just as my right hand was coming up from behind him to block the shot. My right hand – in particular, my right thumb – and his elbow met rather unceremoniously and with great force. Let me tell you that a thumb stands no chance in a one-on-one battle with an elbow. I think I heard a rather loud pop, but I can tell you for sure that I instantly felt lightening shooting through my hand, up my arm, and straight into my head. I looked down at what had once been a very nice thumb and saw a thumb that resembled a painting by Salvador Dali. It was bent and twisted like a Philadelphia pretzel. I picked up my ball, jumped in the car and headed to the house, which thankfully was only a minute or two away. I had to drive one handed and in intense pain, but I made it.

I got home and told my dad that I needed to get to an emergency room fast. He took one look and off we went with barely a word spoken. We got to the emergency room and the real fun began. My thumb wasn't broken, but it was dislocated pretty badly. The emergency room was staffed by a very nice doctor, but she must have weighed 90 pounds max. I mention that because she proceeded to try to pop my thumb back in place – several times – but with no success. She just didn't have the strength or leverage. I had worked up a pretty good sweat while I was on the court and, with the onset of the pain from the dislocation, I was as slippery as a politician taking a bribe. Given her small stature and my overall slippery nature, she could not get the thumb to pop back in place.

The doctor paused. She knew this wasn't working. The pain was immense and I was praying that she could just pop it out. I knew that meant a huge burst of pain as it popped back in place but I was willing to suffer that short-term explosion of pain versus my current condition.

The doctor turned to me and said we will need to operate. These were not the words I wanted to hear. She told the nurse to give me an injection for the pain. I thought, *why the hell didn't you do that before you started pulling on my thumb?* The shot came and the pain resided to a mere fire, as opposed to the volcanic pain I had been experiencing.

I had to sit and wait for the hospital to organize a surgical team and get an operating room ready. By then it is 8 o'clock at night, and they had to call in some of the team for the surgery. I waited and the pain started to gain strength, its embers growing hotter and hotter.

Finally, we got to the operating room and the team did their thing. I was awake, but they gave me a local anesthesia, and I didn't feel too much. The surgical team was in a real jovial mood, I remember that. They were laughing and joking all during the procedure. After they finished, a member of the team held my hand over head. It was in a cast to mid-forearm. He said to me, "I want you to take your thumb and touch your nose with it."

"Sure," I said. "No problem."

He let my hand go and it fell toward my face, like a meteor falling from the sky. I had no control of it at all. It was an inch or so away from my face, when he caught it and said. "This is to show you that you will not have control of your arm for around six hours or so, don't try to move it." He was laughing as he said this. I told you they were in a great mood. They had probably been out drinking for all I know.

I said, "I got it. I got it."

And he was right, I didn't have muscle control over it for some time. But what he didn't tell me is that the pain would come back way before I could move it. It was extremely weird. I could feel the pain all right, burning and throbbing like a hot poker was inside the cast, but I could not move the hand. Finally, blissfully, I fell asleep. When I awoke, the pain was manageable and I could move my hand. I had my hand in a cast for about four weeks and, when it came off, I was pretty much as good as new. A nice little basketball story, huh?

Basketball Story #5

Years later, I met up with one of my basketball teammates from high school who did go on to play at the college level, and he said something that really jolted me. We were having lunch and he said, "Brad, I was so angry at you in high school."

"Why?" I said.

"Because you had so much more talent than I did and you wasted it."

I told him I never knew that he felt that way and that I just never had the drive that he had to succeed to the next level. I had done the math and, even if I pushed as hard as I could in high school, I was never making the pros. It was just not going to happen, so I pushed myself in other areas. But he had a point. I could have gone a bit further and there is a part of me that wishes I had.

Basketball Story #6

About 10 years ago, my friend Dan asked me to join him at a neighborhood gym where they played pickup games. I had not played a full-court game in some time, but figured it would be fun. We got to the gym and watched a game or two before it was our team's turn. I watched the games and I was not impressed. I turned to Dan and said, "These guys suck!"

Eventually, our team got on the court. The moves I made back in high-school came back to me and I was hitting a few shots, but everything seemed to happen in slow motion. I drove down the lane hoping to get to the basket and it was like moving in molasses. When I was in high school, I could play above the rim – not any longer. After a couple of games, I turned to Dan and said, "Dan, guess what? I suck." He smiled.

My high school basketball picture – not a ton
of talent but a lot of hair on my head.

You've Got to Know When to Fold Them

As a teenager, Friday night basically meant one thing and one thing only – poker. It's a cliché, I suppose, and one could argue that we really should have been out on a date, but that was the tradition and we pretty much stuck with it for a couple of years.

The games would last late into the night, and on a couple of occasions well into Saturday morning. Things would get weirder and weirder the longer we played with the games eventually becoming incredibly stupid as time progressed. There was a scene on an old "Star Trek" episode where Kirk discusses a made-up card game call Fizzbin and explains the rules. Fizzbin's rules were bizarre and as our card games wore on into the night, the games seemed to come closer to Fizzbin than to real poker.

One night, it was quite late, and we were playing a truly stupid game called "Acey-Deucey." It is not really poker, but simply guessing if the next card turned up will fall between the preceding two cards flipped up. If the first two cards are say a five and a 10, you would bet whether the next card will fall between that or not. That night, Rich Kosoff and Richard Cohen were locked in a battle in this stupid game and Kosoff kept losing. I mean he lost everything he had and then borrowed from me and lost that as well. I eventually had to call a stop and tell Richard Cohen that Kosoff was no longer responsible for his actions, as he had temporarily lost all capacity for rational thought.

When you start losing on practically sure bets, you should understand that the Poker Gods are not going to let you win that night and know to get the hell out of there. I am not sure how much Rich lost that night but whatever it was, it was more than he could afford to lose, and Richard Cohen was laughing all the way to the bank with Rich's money – and mine for that matter. We should have found a date for that night.

A Boxer Rebellion

I am 20 and attending Temple University. I am studying Political Science and decide to take a summer course at the Ambler campus, a small Temple extension campus in the suburbs. The first day of class arrives and I go in. I scan the class to see if I know anyone and to see who I want to sit next to. I spot a nice-looking girl and sit down next to her. *Why not*, I figure, *it's always worth a shot.*

The class is on the American presidency and it is fairly interesting as these things go. The girl next to me, however, seems less interested than I am. I casually ask her after class if she is a Political Science major and she says, "No way, I am taking this class to fill a Humanities requirement. I am Pre-Med." That explains her obvious lack of interest.

I tell her if she needs any help, just let me know. One or two more classes pass and eventually one thing leads to another and I ask her out. She agrees, and we go out to dinner after class. It is a nice summer evening and we go over to a local restaurant not far from campus. The date is progressing nicely and then she tells me that she is in the midst of breaking up with her old boyfriend. I say something like, "Sorry to hear that." She tells me that he will not take no for answer. She has tried to end it several times, but he keeps coming back to her place and banging at the door and begging her for another chance. At least this is her side of the story.

She says that he is very possessive, and I start to wonder why she is telling all of this on our first date. This seems a bit odd to me. She then lays out the thing she has been dancing around for the last 10 or 15 minutes. She says that she is not 100 percent sure how she still feels about him, but that she is very interested in me as well. This is starting to get more complicated. Then she lays out the final piece of the puzzle. Her current/ex-boyfriend is a professional boxer named Marvis Frazier. I know who Marvis Frazier is. He is the son of heavyweight legend Joe Frazier and is a very good heavyweight boxer in his own right. The date ends shortly after this final revelation.

She calls me a couple of days later. She asks me if we are going to go out again. I say, I don't think so. At this point, she brings up the racial aspect of the situation.

"Are you saying no because I am black?" she asks.

"No, I am saying I don't want to get involved with your situation because your boyfriend is a heavyweight boxer with some obviously strong feelings for you and I don't want him banging on my door in the middle of the night."

I am strong, athletic and confident, but not stupid. I know this has dumb written all over it. The following several classes are a bit, shall we say, uncomfortable, and I decide to sit in a different seat in the back. She gives me the occasional look that says, *you are a wimp*. I can handle that. I got an "A" in the class and she (I guess) got to keep her professional boxer boyfriend. I also got to keep my face intact.

Here is a historical fact: Marvis Frazier only lost two fights in his career. He lost to Larry Holmes in 1983 and Mike Tyson in 1986. I do not believe Brad Center would also have been on that list of losses.

Note: For those of you not as familiar with world history, there was an uprising in China between 1899 and 1901 called the Boxer Rebellion. The jokes are funnier if you've taken the proper course prerequisites before attempting the read this book. I'm just saying.

Uncle Lou

I am 17, and since it's summertime, my brother and I are doing a stint as camp counselors at Camp Arthur/Reeta when we get a call one afternoon that our Uncle Lou has died. The call hit me like a surreal punch in the gut from God.

My uncle had heart issues and had recently undergone bypass surgery, but my Uncle Lou was so full of life that, even though intellectually I understood that his passing was not an impossibility, it just didn't square with the man I had experienced in the last few months. I was not the only one devastated by the loss of Louis Frantz. My Aunt Jan was crushed. This was her love and true companion, and she has never found another person who measured up to my Uncle Lou. My cousins Niles, Adam, and Barbara had to work through the loss of a caring and dedicated father and a man that was truly an inspiration to them and to many others as well.

The family gathered, as families do at these times. As a young man, I recall the impact it had on not just Niles, Adam, and Barb, but on all my cousins. We were a fairly close-knit family back then. You know how it is, the family gathers for Thanksgiving dinner and all the cousins end up at the kids table. You bond and share good times together, but you also come together as a group during times like this. So here we were – my brother and I, with Karen, Andi, Jackie, Michael, Steven, and Sheryl – all gathered together, sharing not only our collective grief but also in the fond memories that bound us together.

As I look back on that event, I know how it shaped me, molded me, and transformed me. My Uncle Lou's passing was the first death that truly impacted me. I started to understand loss in a basic and primal way. I took away from this the life lessons one might expect: 1) Life is short, it goes by in a blink; 2) The future is unknown and unknowable; 3) We need to cherish those we love and the time we have with them.

But more than that, I began to understand the absolute finality of life. I began to see how the darkness that is death reaches deep into our souls. It resides there, not in any overt way, but it is there and we know it. So, we strive and we push, each in our own way, to leave some kind of imprint on a world that will eventually move on without us. That is not a bad thing, nor is it a good thing, but rather it is just the way that it is. There is not too much more to say except that I loved my Uncle Lou and still love his spirit to this day.

"I do love nothing in the world so well as you." (Much Ado About Nothing, Act IV, Scene I)

I was 17 and a senior in high school and I hated advanced mathematics. It is ultimately my disdain for higher math that lead me to meeting Valerie Hauser who, years later, would become Valerie Center, my wife of more than 26 years and counting.

I met Valerie in a class called Math Survey. I was in 12th grade and I had taken Algebra I and Algebra II and Geometry, but there was no way I was taking Calculus. I would rather stick a needle in my eye (and yes, I have had that happen – two cataract surgeries and four detached retinas). So instead of Calculus, I found this silly little class called Math Survey. I also found my soulmate – not a bad call if I do say so myself.

Here is where I am supposed to say it was love at first sight, and that's probably true for me but it took Val a little longer. I have never met a person who better understands me than Val. What is amazing is that she loves me anyway!

Val and I sat next to each other in Math Survey and the rapport was immediate as was the attraction – at least for me. As I said, it took Val longer to fall in love with me – about 10 years longer. Math Survey was not exactly a rigorous class, and Val and I found time for silly stuff. One of games we played to amuse ourselves was to try to get our teacher (Mrs. Ruskin) to say very strange words or phrases during the class. At the beginning of the class we would select a word, for example *Egypt*, as the word of the day and our challenge would be to get Mrs. Ruskin to say that exact word sometime during the 50-minute class. We would obviously be forced to lead her on and ask her stupid questions like, "Yes, I understand that mathematical principle but would that same principle apply in Egypt?" She would hopefully, respond with something like, "What? Why wouldn't it apply in Egypt?" Mission Accomplished! She must have thought we were nuts.

Now I must admit to being a bad influence on Valerie. She was naturally a dedicated student, and though I had been one myself, when we got together I was naturally distracted, and I managed to distract her during the class as much as possible. Near the end of the year and close to our graduation, things started to deteriorate and studying became a bit of an afterthought to the point where we both managed to get a 12 on a test – that is a 12 out of a 100, just to be clear. Neither of us had ever gotten lower than a "C" on a test before in high school, so this was a major accomplishment – just not one you tended to brag about. Mrs. Ruskin was dumbfounded. She handed back the tests and made a sarcastic comment saying, "I would suspect you of cheating off each other because you both managed to get a 12 but you got different things wrong. That is quite a talent you two have." We tended to dumfound her quite a bit. I think I got a "B" as my final grade for the class. Val probably got an "A" even after receiving the 12 on that one test. I told you she was a naturally good student.

I was such a bad influence on Val during that year that I managed to persuade her to cut our Math Survey class one spring morning. We went to a nearby restaurant called the Red Lion Diner. This was the first time Valerie had ever cut a class, so she was a bit nervous about the whole thing. We had breakfast and watched a young waitress drop a whole tray of dishes that shattered on the diner floor. Val was so nervous at cutting class that she nearly jumped out of her seat as the dishes crashed to the floor.

Anyway, that is how I met my wife of 26 years – based on an aversion to advanced mathematics!

Science Fiction

I began my love affair with Valerie in 12th grade, but a year earlier I started another long-lasting relationship with science fiction. Admittedly, this is a different kind of love, but I liked the segue, so deal with it.

About the same time, I met two people who I still call friends to this day. I met Howard Maunus and Gary Schaaf in English class, and we naturally started hanging out together. Our 11th grade English teacher (Mr. Goldman) asked us to develop a paper on the founding fathers of science fiction. We had to select two authors and do a short biography and then write a summary of one of their famous works.

Well, to cut down on the work load, we focused our research on just one of the authors and handed off that research to each other. I selected H.G. Wells as my research topic, Gary picked George Orwell, and Howard took Aldous Huxley. When it came time to write the essays, we relied on each other's research for our second author. For example, I did Wells and Orwell, using the research Gary had done on Orwell. Gary did Orwell, but also wrote on Huxley using the research Howard did on Huxley, and so on. At least, I think that is how it went down. The plan required a great deal of trust and it worked. It cemented our friendship and we each got excellent grades on our essays, so it was truly a win/win. Our teacher was none the wiser.

However, to my mind, I was the luckiest one of all. I got hooked on science fiction. After we handed in those essays, I began to read every piece of science fiction I could find. I quickly devoured everything in the George Washington High School library and then started going to other libraries and bookstores. I have read thousands of science fiction and speculative fiction books over the years, but it all started with Huxley, Wells, and Orwell. Thank you, Mr. Goldman.

Your Actual Highway Mileage My Vary

The story that follows shows either how incredibly stupid I am (Rich Kosoff as well) or how much God looks down from above to protect the purely moronic of this world. Judge for yourself.

It was somewhere around 1983. Rich had moved out to Los Angeles a few years earlier, and I came out for a visit. Part of the trip included a short jaunt out to Vegas for a couple of nights. We did the usual: gambled, saw a couple of shows, and hung out at the pool. We had a good time and, oddly enough the stupid aspect of this story does not occur in Vegas and does not include, alcohol, women, or drugs.

We left Vegas early in the morning for the drive back to L.A. The drive takes about four and a half hours. We left very early and there was no one on the road – literally no one. We were on Route 15, which is dead straight and, like I said, the road was empty. Rich was driving. We hadn't gotten too far when Rich let me know he was tired. Now, the intelligent thing to do at this point and time would have been to pull over and switch, letting me get behind the wheel. For reasons that escape me some thirty years later, this is not what we decided to do.

I took the wheel from the passenger side and then stuck my left leg across the mid-section of the car and held down the accelerator to keep the car at 55. Needless to say, the car did not have cruise control. Rich went to sleep and I held the wheel (quick aside, Rich's super power is the ability to fall asleep in seconds anytime he is tired). I steered the car for around 20 to 30 minutes. The road stayed empty and Rich slept on. Eventually my left arm started to ache and my leg started to cramp. I turned to Rich and said, "Wake up, dude." Nothing. He kept right on sleeping. I waited a minute or so and again called over to him to wake up and again nothing. The boy can sleep. At this point, my arm and leg were too fatigued to go on in their current positions, so in a much louder voice I yelled over to Rich to wake the fuck up.

He jumped in his seat. He had no idea where he was. All he knew was that he was behind the wheel of a car flying down the highway and his hands were not actually anywhere near the wheel. His hands flew up to grab the wheel, practically driving us off the road into a ditch. He said, "What the fuck? Where are we?"

I reminded him what had transpired about 45 minutes ago. He cleared his head and said, "Thanks, I got it." I rubbed my aching arm and pulled my leg back to the correct side of the car. We continued the trip back to L.A. – Rich, me, and some kind guardian angel riding in the back.

PART 7

Poetry Interlude

Okay, folks, time for a little break. High school is over, and I am about to enter adulthood. But, before I do that, I wanted to pass along some poetry I've written over the years. For you uncultured miscreants, you can skip over the next dozen pages or so, but do you really want to be branded as a philistine?

This book comes with a hidden microchip that feeds back specific data to me – the pages you've read, those that you skip, etc. So, I will know if you pass by these literary gems, these works of art, and I will be forced to hunt you down, knock on your door, and read them out loud to you. Do you want that to happen?

We will begin this little poetic journey with a piece I composed rather recently. My wife's sister passed away, and Val wanted a poem to read at the service. Here is what came forth:

A Life

Deep warm waters roll slowly without much purpose or cause
The ethereal void descends and a gentle wind caresses
Imperceptible movement begins

Sluggishly the ocean moans
The wind a mid-wife to yet another watery traveler
No thought, just desire as a journey commences

Green to azure and back again
Momentum gains – and a sailboat gently rises and falls
Her presence holds and the world rolls out before her

The shore approaches
Time to move to grow to churn
Careless, driven, energetic – there is no other way

She moves as she must
She rises, she crests – proud, jubilant, alive
A pause, the descent, and then life spreads thin

So thin, oh so very, very thin
Dissolving and folding back
Back to everything and nothing and to everything

This one was obviously not written while I was in the most upbeat of moods, but I like it.

Survival

Silent sky, grey and sullen
enveloping all, and my senses were never told
entry without intrusion
no message is clear in the mist

Dawn, but who can tell
who has fallen in the night
shards of sanity litter the streets
clouds filled with indifference burst and wash them away

Momentum spins the day along
our pockets are pulled inside out
eyes, ears, and mouth useless
covered and clogged with a film milky and white

Days, black and hollow
surviving each moment until
the next comes along
Place your hand upon me   Let it end.

These next two were written upon request as wedding gifts:

Living in the Mist

Descending upon your souls
Blurring the boundary between thoughts and emotion
Reality and illusion merge
And Monet's perspective hides in your eye.

Ethereal, untouchable, yet ever present
A feathery embrace of pastoral memories
Extending to you no clarity
For clarity is no gift here.

Holding together what was once held apart
It offers depth, where none seems possible
And offers insight even while you cannot see
Sustenance for the soul.

Nothing to grasp in this formless enigma
Moving towards the uncertainty principle
A quantum entity materialized
Art, science, and spirit unify.

What it was like before this – you cannot say
Nor can you even remember
No intent or design are needed
Only an invitation to remain.

To the Goddess

It exists
If nothing else know this
It exists

To the shrine the multitudes have come
Their coffers laden with gold
But the hunger in their eyes
Made their sacrifices unworthy

They knew you by many names
Although you have but one nature
Every age has called out to you

Aphrodite, daughter of Zeus
Sacred myrtle in your hand, desire flowing from your lips
Rati, wife of Kama
All the games which speak Love's name, are seen through you

Var, Astarte, Frigg, and Hathor
I know you whispered into Aesop's ear when he wrote the Lion's tale
From which we know that even the wildest can be tamed by love

You are eternal
Your power infinite
Your champions – Percy, Shelly, Keats, and Browning
Your prophets – Gibran, Balzac, Moliere, and Voltaire – each have done
you justice
In eloquence they proclaimed that Love is a canvass, furnished by Nature,
and embroidered by imagination

The threads of history tell the tale
What color thread is yours?
Is it white – innocent and absolute?
Is it red – colored from our heart and our pain?

You compel us onward to a fate we do not know
Nor can we even comprehend
But like the pilgrim in search of a shrine
We come willingly into your arms

Poetry and Politics

Hostage

Poisoned bars rusted brown by time's indifferent passage. Still the stagnant stench of captivity cannot escape its defenses. A footstep echoes off into infinity.

And I wonder when I'll be home again and the moon-rise answers never.

Awakened by morning's din, to words foreign and strange. And I've asked and asked again, for what purpose can this serve. They feed me but nothing more.

And I ache to breathe you in.

Desperation fills their faces. Perhaps the time is near. One way or another I'll be free.

Days in Sand

Day 1
Light dies upon the horizon
Men soiled and tired press on
Taking pipe they open earth's crust
Following sins haunting song
Desires so large they're used for fuel
They become machines of unthinking men

Day 2
Sands of the Sahara fly fierce
And soon others join the quest
Pumped with pride and petulance
They display their muddied crest
Desert flesh splits apart
As liquid spews forth from a heart that's pierced

Day 3
In secret service to a force unsaid
A desire with no cure
Futile attempts are made
To draw lines on the desert floor
The thirst grows stronger and
Needed fuel turns from black to red

And I, as tired as can be, feel nothing.

This one is a little out there. The tortured angst-ridden soul type of thing.

One Alone

Thundering over the horizon,
astride a steed of white
speaking simple truths,
with a sword pure and clean
to battle with Glory and Passion – Right is clear
Suddenly awakened: our eyes fall open

Stadium screams, hallway accusations
rumors, and innuendo
fragmented, alienated and so alone,
Betrayed by a lover's kiss

Traveling by himself,
his feet pound on desert sand
down a path unclear,
with methods unsure
he is scared and untested
Too much seen today
and not enough perceived of yesterday

A dust storm clouds his eyes,
his skin is seared and peels
it begins to pour, hard unyielding raindrops
his sight is deluded in refraction
The mob gets angry and then grows weary

They close their eyes and fall asleep

It has been a long time since I wrote the poem below. I was in a strange mood when I composed it.

Submerged

Sea winds touch flesh
Tickling the skin with sensation
Lighter than the light
Breathing deep before the plunge

Soft liquid, warm and calm
surround the soul and comfort
Spinning, twisting a playful spirit
An otter awash in a new universe

Curiosity knows no limit
un-oceaning treasures in crevice and crag
Creatures alight in colors bold
They dart and squirt without plan or future
Knowing only the inch of universe before them

Forces beyond the senses,
beyond comprehension,
light and life now fade
Motions & thoughts
deaden in a night
deeper than the
darkness

Home

I think the title kind of says it all on this one.

Between Pilate's Lashes

1... Oh GOD -- Stung by a viper's tongue ...2

3... Hungry eyes, seeking love, weakness, forgiveness ...4

5... Please let me be, let me go home -- this is not fair ...6

7... Dripping down my back flows burning lava -- my soul ...8

9... The pain! I'm lost, disconnected ...10

11... Searing, slicing, burning -- WHERE ARE YOU? ...12

13... Feel it burn, their hate and fear ...14

15... I am calling, watching life slipping away ...16

17... Why am I here? What purpose can this serve? ...18

19... Circuits fuse, overloaded, flesh tingles ...20

21... Night folds its wings and descends ...22

23... TAKE ME AWAY ...24

25... Blackness, falling -- nothing until ...26

27... Glowing eyes alight inside ...28

29... Blackening my soul -- turn away ...30

31... End this now or enter eternity's darkness ...32

33... Release myself ...34

35... Let go the mind -- find and gain the heart ...36

37... TAKE ME BACK HOME ...38

39... SURRENDER TO THE PAIN, SURRENDER TO YOU ...

A couple of poems about love's journey

Seduction

Silence, then a rumbling crash upon the shore
Silence again, the ocean sighs
Release, energy gushes forth out of the womb of life
Again the ocean sighs

You stand silent, in awe
Contemplating a relationship you are just beginning to grasp
Comforting – it is easy to stand apart, so near, yet safe

A lover calling, you turn away
You run from the power and intensity, but again you stop and listen…
Don't you see we are one?
I am part of you
I'm the secret in the heart of your soul
"I burn inside your soul"

Stand back, too close risks the pull…
We are destiny
Be fulfilled as I surround you

A step, then another, water of life touches and caresses you
A chill spreads throughout you
Found by an everlasting love
And again the ocean sighs

Back to You Again

Awake from a fitful sleep...
words and phrases veiled behind the mist of slumber,
they hover just beyond reach and understanding.

A voice whispers within the night. A thousand faces in a day's reality. A promise remains as yet unfulfilled. A head turns skyward in a gesture of confusion and pain, winds blow, a chill spreads, and he knows it is not yet time.

They talk and the hours pass by and take no notice. He starts to wonder – as his heart skips a beat and begins again. He begins to live in the moment of anticipation and suddenly, over the edge, he falls.

The time is too soon. Destiny's doors will not budge. He thrashes and pounds, his hands bloody and raw – turning away, the traveler ascends.

Another enters in similar fashion, obsessed by a symbol he represents. They join in a silent struggle to stem the avalanche of loneliness. In time the climbers part, each choosing a different route to the summit.

From above he peers below to recognize the voice within the night. He stares amazed and enchanted. It seems the air must be too thin. He waits for her to join him.

A time to rest, as they hold tight. Up ahead, they find a small plateau. Here they pause, until the summit calls and they must leave.

And finally, a poem inspired by an Alan Parsons Project song

The Traveler

My town hangs still in the country air
Morning comes over the hills slowly without much motivation
Mother ushers me out to play
Along the path I travel, going nowhere in particular
I plod on, through the glen
Too sure of events yet unborn
The neighbor's dog trots up and sniffs my pant leg
We run for a minute or two, losing interest we part company
Crossing, at a street with no name
I wave at others, the gesture returned
Their gaze lowers to the ground
The sidewalk echoes with snippets of familiar conversation
I reach the other side – a reflection in the mirror it seems to me
A wind blows from the east and I cast my gaze in that direction
A man walks towards me, pats me on the head
He's tall, quite big, but I like the way he smiles
He talks to me
He's from a place I do not know
I follow him back to town
He talks, the town's people listen with brows furrowed
Slowly they smile, nod and some slap him on the back
He walks on as a steady breeze cools our faces
I do not understand his words too well
But it feels good to walk with him just the same
Night comes and we settle on a hill just above the glen
Stars fill the sky and I watch intently
Our days can be like the stars, infinite and diverse
Watch them closely
One day you'll know where you really are
The dawn comes and he is gone
Where he goes I do not know

Something compels him on
And in my mind I'm not far behind

PART 8

Adulthood

"Like a wind crying endlessly through the universe, time carries away the names and the deeds of conquerors and commoners alike. And all that we were, all that remains, is in the memories of those who cared we came this way for a brief moment."

— Harlan Ellison

Introduction: The following stories are all true and factual except for the parts that aren't -- those are completely fictitious. Enjoy. . .

The Supremes

I am 24 and in graduate school at American University in Washington D.C. My friend Pete is in his first year of law school at American. Pete gets an invitation (don't ask me how) to attend the Red Mass in Washington D.C. So off we go.

While there are many Red Mass services around the world, the one in Washington D.C. is somewhat special as it attracts the Supreme Court justices. A Red Mass is celebrated by the Catholic Church and requests guidance from the Holy Spirit for those in the legal profession. Unlike a certain Red Wedding – nobody is killed. I believe the term Red Mass comes from the color of the robes worn by the royal judges in eras gone by – but what do I know? I am a Jewish kid from Philly.

The Red Mass is celebrated at the Cathedral of St. Matthew the Apostle. It is a very beautiful church. We arrive, and Pete is gracious enough to guide me through the ceremony because I've never attended a Catholic mass before in my life. I find the whole thing fascinating, ornate, and full of traditions I know little about, but I watch and learn.

Out of the corner of my eye, I spot three Supreme Court justices to include the chief justice himself. The Mass ends and we adjourn to a private club known as the John Carroll Society. Peter and I mingle. I have no clue who 90% of the people are, but they appear to be some very powerful people. They speak in hushed tones and carry themselves with an air of authority and purpose. I am impressed.

We wander upstairs and find ourselves in the library. In walks the one of the justices. We introduce ourselves, and he nods. He turns and inelegantly trips over a potted plant on the floor and the masque of authority and sophistication suddenly vanishes. It is a fake plant and that is fairly obvious – at least to everyone but the justice. He begins to gather himself up from the floor with our assistance. He starts fussing over the plant, still convinced it is a real plant. Pete and I give each other a look that says, "This man is part of the highest court of the land. This is not good." We pretend the plant is real to placate the justice and let him know that we will gladly handle the situation and make sure the plant is alright.

I look around, and suddenly the façade of power seems to dissolve around me. I see people, well-dressed people, but just people. It is a lesson; I plan to remember.

The story I just told was not meant to embarrass a justice of the Supreme Court who I have not named but who you could easily look up. The individual in question had a distinguished career. Rather, I tell it because of the incongruity of the story and how we tend to look at titles not people.

Bumpkins

I am 25 and it turns out I am a bumpkin. For those unfamiliar with the term, the dictionary defines bumpkin as *an unsophisticated or socially awkward person from the countryside.* That's the end of the story but let me turn on the "Way-Back" machine (thank you Mr. Peabody and Sherman) and let's see how it turns out that I am a bumpkin even though I am not socially awkward or from the country.

To begin this tale, I must introduce two people – Jim and Steve. I met both Jim and Steve in graduate school, and I have remained friends with Jim ever since. Steve moved to South America and I have long since lost touch with him. While in graduate school, Jim, Steve, and I had an internship at a major government agency. We had the esteemed pleasure of working for a man whose management style resembled that of Attila the Hun. I am not going to speak kindly of this individual, who shall remain nameless. I will simply call him Mr. Hun, after Attila the Hun. Let's do that. So, the preceding "esteemed pleasure" statement was meant to contain as much dripping sarcasm as I can jam into those two words. If sarcasm was a natural resource as prevalent as oil, there would not be enough sarcasm on the earth to accurately reflect how much I want to pour into those two words.

Here is the story. Jim, Steve, and I had been working as interns there for a couple of months. One day, all three of us were a bit late coming into the office, not tremendously late, just 30 minutes or so but we were technically late. This occurred, oddly enough, on a morning when Mr. Hun wanted to see us, as a group, to espouse on some topic or other. He wanted an audience and we, being interns, were a perfect audience for whatever profundity (there's that sarcasm again) he wanted to share. The only problem was, we weren't there. Mr. Hun flipped.

When we arrived in the office, we were summoned to Mr. Hun's office. Mr. Hun was a large round man and his face was crimson red. He was darn near apoplectic. He couldn't even speak for a few minutes, he just paced back and forth. Finally, he turned to the three of us and said, "Do you know what you guys are? Do you know?" We sat silently because we knew this was a rhetorical question and Mr. Hun was certainly going to tell us what we were.

"You're bumpkins, all three of you. I thought long and hard on that before saying it. You guys are bumpkins. Do you think you can casually just waltz in here anytime you darn well feel like it?"

Again, we remained silent. Speaking at a time like this would only further stoke his fire, and it looked like he was about to have a stroke as it was. I should point out that the lecture went on for a good 15 minutes or so, focused almost entirely on our "bumpkiness." He was loud and angry and so we sat silently and then, at the end, promised it would never happen again.

We left Mr. Hun's office, heads hung appropriately low, and walked back to our office. When we got there, we burst out laughing. Yes, that's right, we started laughing. We knew Mr. Hun for what he was (pompous and a bit self-righteous) but were dumbfounded by the bumpkin comment. We just stood there laughing. We just got called bumpkins! We were ready for just about anything but that. We knew we were wrong for being late and were expecting to be called out in some sane way for that offense, but the oddity of the bumpkin comment caught us off-guard. We held in the laughter until we got back to our office but then the dam burst.

I would also point out that for three bumpkins, we all did okay. As I said, I lost track of Steve, but he was living down in South America devoting a lot of time to worthy causes in some very poor countries. Jim, who is one of the smartest guys I have ever met, works as a Director at Deloitte, has four kids, and is also a caring and decent man. His only fault is that he is probably smarter than me, but I like him enough to let that pass. As for me, I hope to prove my "non-bumpkiness" at every possible moment.

Machismo

I am 27 years old and living with my friend Jim in Arlington, Virginia. We were working in the federal government for a program called the Presidential Management Intern (PMI), later renamed the Presidential Management Fellow program. It was, and still is, a fairly prestigious program, and we were happy be selected. We worked hard but also liked to go out and have a good time on the weekends. We were young, single and had a lot of energy back then.

Jim was a natural in the club scene. I mentioned how smart he is, but he is also a good-looking guy. Bars and clubs are made for people like Jim. Luckily, he is a great guy because between his intellect and good looks, I would have had plenty of reasons to dislike him.

We would occasionally visit a club in Arlington called The Pawn Shop. The Pawn Shop is long gone, but we both remember it well. The Pawn Shop had its share of regulars, and I guess we could be counted as part of that crowd. One of the other regulars was a guy straight out of Central Casting in 1977, that we nicknamed "Machismo." Machismo wore silk shirts unbuttoned to expose his chest. He wore gold chains and basically looked like he was an extra from the Saturday Night Fever movie. Unfortunately for Machismo, time had continued to move forward and it was no longer 1977, and other than John Travolta, people really didn't dress like that even back then. Well, maybe a few did, but trust me, they shouldn't have.

Machismo played his part perfectly, and by that, I mean he was comical and a tad pathetic in his approach. He came on loud and strong with every woman in the bar. He didn't care how many times he got shot down. While comical, I did feel a bit bad for him. It was a train wreck, but it was hard not to watch. Let us take our leave of Machismo for a minute; I promise we will return to him shortly.

It was the summer of 1986 and Jim and I decided to throw a party. Jim had only recently bought the condo we lived in, and we needed to celebrate. In other words, this seemed like a good excuse to throw a big bash. We pulled out all the stops and invited just about everyone we knew. Included in the list of invites was an old girl-friend of mine (we will call her Caterina just because I like the way the name sounds, although this was not her real name).

All the invites went out, and we got the place ready for the party. I didn't think of Caterina again until she walked through the door the night of the party. Now, let's pause and say that Caterina, was a smart, attractive woman and while we were no longer dating, I thought she had good taste. She dated me after all (I assume everyone knew that line was coming). To my shock, horror, and incredible amusement, Caterina walks in the door, arm-in-arm, with none other than Machismo!

How did they meet? I have no idea. Why was Caterina with him? I have no idea. Why does time slow as you approach the speed of light? I actually kind of understand that one, but more about time dilation theory later on. This stuff with Caterina was beyond comprehension. She was with Machismo and acting as if such a thing were not against the laws of nature as I had come to understand them! Jim and I gaped but kept our composure. We welcomed them into the house and then made some excuse and ducked into a nearby bedroom to collect ourselves. We burst out laughing and kept saying, "It's Machismo, and he is in our house." We must have said it a dozen times, trying to get our heads around the absurdity of the situation

I did my best to avoid Caterina and Machismo the rest of the night, as looking at them together made me doubt my own reality and generally left me tongue-tied and flabbergasted. I decided that alcohol would be the most appropriate coping mechanism. I drank ¾ of a bottle of tequila that night. It helped.

To this day, all you have to do is say the word "machismo," and Jim and I will crack a smile and think back to the day he came into our home with my ex-girlfriend. The world is a strange place.

Movie Time

I love movies. I love how they can draw you into a world that you didn't know existed before you entered the theater. I love how characters you never knew just hours before can fill your heart and mind. I love how they can make you see, think, and feel something new. Of course, all of that is only true when the movie is done well, with great care, and with people who have talent and care about their craft. So, let's take a moment to salute the best of the best in this genre. Here are my favorites (as best as my memory can recall). I will try to summarize each selection in a sentence or so. Let me know what you think. Tell me you like my selections. Tell me you think I am nuts. Or think of it this way – here are over 100 reasons to call me crazy. Let's begin.

Classics

1. "Citizen Kane" – It's a classic and a must see but I will admit it is a bit of an acquired taste.
2. "12 Angry Men" – A great play and film. The acting is superb.
3. "Casablanca" – A bit dated, but still a good film.
4. "The African Queen" – I like Bogart and Hepburn – need I say more?
5. "North by Northwest" – Hard to pick from the many Hitchcock films but this one is interesting, and I like Cary Grant.

Comedies

1. "Monty Python and the Holy Grail" – Simply funny every second of the film.
2. "Groundhog Day" – Bill Murry and holidays work for me.
3. "Young Frankenstein" – My favorite Mel Brooks film with so many quotable lines.
4. "The Princess Bride" – I love this film and again tons of quotable lines.
5. "Joe Versus the Volcano" – Most people do not share my love for this quirky little film, but it was the first pairing of Meg Ryan and Tom Hanks and it works for me and Val.
6. "Annie Hall" – The list needs at least one Woody Allen film.

7. "Scrooged" – Bill Murry is the movie.

8. "Heathers" – I love good dark comedy.

9. "Arthur" – Just a good solid comedy; also, some good quotable lines.

10. "When Harry Met Sally" – Meg is great, and it is kind of how I found my wife.

11. "Good Morning, Vietnam" – Robin Williams needed to be represented.

12. "Raising Arizona" – Maybe not to everyone's taste but is very well done.

13. "The Producers" – The original with Zero Mostel and Gene Wilder

14. "Ferris Bueller's Day Off "– A classic 80's comedy

15. "Ghostbusters" – So many quotable lines

16. "Animal House" – Anyone from my generation has this on their list.

17. "Blazing Saddles" – Another Mel Brooks classic

18. "Play it Again, Sam" – Another strong Woody Allen film

19. "Trading Places" – Again, anyone from my generation should have this on their list.

20. "Planes, Trains and Automobiles" – Steve Martin and John Candy, need I say more?

21. "Roxanne" – Most likely not on everyone's list, but I do like this film. (Quotable Line involves the phrase, "Earn more sessions by sleeving")

22. "Airplane!" – Stupid and inane, but still funny

23. "Beetlejuice" – Screw Keaton as Batman. This is him at his best.

Westerns

1. "Unforgiven" – A good, realistic western

2. "Silverado" – The complete opposite of "Unforgiven," fun but not to be taken too seriously.

3. "Butch Cassidy and the Sundance Kid" – This one makes the list just for the scene where they jump off the cliff.

4. "Maverick" – True, it really has some unbelievable plot twists, but I think it works regardless.

5. "The Quick and the Dead" – Sharon Stone looks great in a cowboy hat.
6. "Cat Ballou" – OK, it's really dumb, but I am including it anyway.
7. "The Good, the Bad and the Ugly" – A classic spaghetti western
8. "Paint Your Wagon" – How many westerns are also musicals?

Science Fiction

1. "Gattaca" – A great and well-done film
2. "Dr. Strangelove" – Nobody better argue with this selection.
3. "ET" – This movie gets major points for one simple reason, they never tried to do a sequel and thereby ruin the memory.
4. "The Abyss" – It has science fiction elements to it but works even without the sci fi parts
5. 2001: A Space Odyssey" and "2010" – Both are very good but for totally different reasons.
6. "The Truman Show" – I think this is a strong, well done flick.
7. "Ex Machina" – Great dialogue and acting
8. "Terminator 2: Judgement Day" – Better than the first and better than all of the other sequels (I have lost count).
9. "Blade Runner" – One of the best, and a standard bearer for good science fiction films.
10. "The Martian" – Any film that attempts to get gravity right works for me; so many films have people standing around on a spaceship – how?
11. "Close Encounters of the Third Kind" – Dreyfus, a good script, and some good special effects that still work today make this a great film.
12. "Looper" – No one ever really gets time travel right in the movies, but it is a fun ride nevertheless.
13. "Déjà Vu" – Starring Denzel Washington, this film is not known by many but it should be.
14. "I Am Legend" – A good film but did they really have to kill off the dog?
15. "Being John Malkovich" – Too weird for some, but just weird enough for me.

16. "Silent Running" – Back in the early '70s they made a little-known film about space and ecology, and when you add Bruce Dern, it works well.
17. "Children of Men" – Depressing, but a well-done film.
18. "The Andromeda Strain" – Nobody with a brain would not have this on their list.
19. "The Time Traveler's Wife" – A nice film that focuses more on the characters than on time travel itself.
20. "Soylent Green" – Edward G Robinson's last film with a great ending.
21. "Contact" – I must admit that I have a bit of a thing for Jodie Foster (see Maverick in westerns.)

War Films
1. "The Boy in the Striped Pajamas" – If you are in the mood to be deeply depressed, this is your film.
2. "Schindler's List" – Of course "Schindler's List" is also terribly depressing, but a masterpiece. I saw this in the theater and at the end of the film, you heard absolutely nothing. No one talked, no one breathed, no one moved until the lights came on.
3. "The Book Thief"– Another great film that shows the savagery of the Nazi regime.
4. "Saving Private Ryan" – One very realistic-looking war movie
5. "The Great Escape" – This is a classic and it has such a great ensemble cast.
6. "The Dirty Dozen" – As unrealistic as a war movie gets but fuck it, I love it.
7. "Full Metal Jacket" – Two films in one, and the first half is riveting.
8. "Platoon" – I can't believe I am including a film with Charlie Sheen, but it is good.
9. "The Killing Fields" – Powerful film
10. "Patton" – Iconic
11. "Apocalypse Now" – The better Sheen in my opinion.

Blood and Guts

1. "V for Vendetta" – Violent science fiction/political intrigue flick, it has all the elements that interest me.
2. "Kill Bill," Volumes I and II – No redeeming social value and I love it.
3. 'Troy" – Admittedly maybe not a truly great film, but it makes the list simply for the great fight scene between Achilles and Hector.
4. "Gladiator" – Nothing like the Romans for some good blood and guts

All Around Great Films

1. "Network" – Perhaps more relevant today than when it was made back in the '70s.
2. "The Natural" – A personal favorite
3. "All That Jazz" – It works on every level.
4. "Jaws" – A film that actually made you jump out of your seat. Screw the sequels.
5. "The Shawshank Redemption" – I will never turn this off when it pops up on TV, I think that says it all.
6. "Defending Your Life" – Not a big believer in an afterlife but if there is one, then this version suits my warped sensibilities.
7. "Raging Bull" – A great De Niro flick
8. "Cinderella Man" – A good root for the underdog kind of film
9. "Rocket Gibraltar" – A great film that pays tribute to family, Jackson Pollock and Viking funerals. What more can you ask for?
10. "Dog Day Afternoon" – Early and fantastic Pacino
11. "Pulp Fiction" – Quentin Taratino's best work, period.
12. "Fight Club" – A bit of an acquired taste, but Edward Norton and Brad Pitt are great or is it just Edward Norton that is great or it just Pitt? Anyway, we can't talk about it!
13. "Forrest Gump" – I wasn't sure if I wanted to include this or not, but in the end, it makes the list because it is a memorable film.
14. "Goodfellas" – My favorite mafia movie.
15. "Dead Poets Society" -- Both inspirational and heartbreaking at the same time

16. "The Silence of the Lambs" – Excellent film, and, yes if we are counting, that is three Jodie Foster films.

17. "A Few Good Men" – Included if only for Nicholson's courtroom speech.

18. "Juno" – Quirky and irreverent enough to make the list.

19. "One Flew Over the Cuckoo's Nest" – Nurse Ratched was the perfect foil for Jack.

20. "Cool Hand Luke" – Paul Newman is, well, just too cool.

21. "Life of Pi" – Visually entertaining and philosophically interesting.

22. "Sideways" – "I am NOT drinking any fucking Merlot!"

23. "The Usual Suspects" – Great acting and fun story combine to make a very good film.

24. "Raiders of the Lost Ark" – I dare anyone not to have this on your list.

25. "Bourne Identity" – A good film that Mr. Kosoff implored me to include.

26. "The Right Stuff" – A great story

27. "Marathon Man" – "Is it safe?"

28. "Whiplash" – I was on the edge of my seat and it is a movie about a drummer – well done.

29. "What Dreams May Come" – Powerful, visually impressive, and touching. Ironic considering how Robin Williams died.

30. "Stand By Me" – Another Stephen King entry, a film that captures what it is like to be young.

31. "Dogma" – Please recommend this to all your most conservative and religious friends – it will go over so well!

32. "Broadcast News" – Funny and profound and works on both levels

33. "Extremely Loud and Incredibly Close" – Helps us make sense of tragedy.

34. "Fences" – Just great acting.

35. "Local Hero" – Quirky, odd, and endearing.

36. "The Big Chill" – A classic

37. "Memento" – It takes a little work, but it is worth it.

38. "Se7en" – "What's in the box?"

39. "Birdman" – Just really well done, and I love the one camera perspective.

40. "Slumdog Millionaire" – One in a million.
41. "Million Dollar Baby" – Make that two in a million.
42. "Crash" – Worth re-watching.
43. "The Deer Hunter" – Timeless.
44. "Boiler Room" – Better than "Glengarry Glen Ross."

Animated (and for some added amusement let's add some kid films)
1. "Wall-E" – Love that little guy.
2. "James and The Giant Peach" – Not as well-known as many but very well done
3. "Aladdin" – Worth it for Robin Williams
4. "Finding Dory" – OK, I admit it, I think Ellen DeGeneres is pretty amusing here.
5. "Toy Story" – A kid's classic
6. "The Jungle Book" – Just perfect
7. "Bambi Meets Godzilla" – Well not exactly a full-length feature, but if you can spare 15 seconds check it out on You Tube. (OK not really a kid film either.)
8. "Wallace and Gromit: The Wrong Trousers" – Another great Nick Park film
9. "Fantasia" – Another iconic film.
10. "The Nightmare Before Christmas" – Fits my twisted sense of humor.
11. "Iron Giant" – A homage to days gone by and possibly Vin Diesel's best role as the Iron Giant.
12. "The Emperor's New Groove" – This dumb film has no reason to be on anyone's list but screw it, Val and I love it and can quote lines from it. Don't ask why.

Movies I Didn't Get
1. "District 9" – Seriously rated as a great Sci Fi film and I found it gross and dumb.
2. "Something About Mary" – Everyone seemed to find this film hysterical; I didn't, not at all.
3. "Dumb and Dumber" – Ditto.

4. "Barton Fink" – Watched wallpaper fall off the wall for like 20 minutes and had to turn it off.

5. "The English Patient" – Highly acclaimed and highly boring.

6. "Mad Max: Fury Road" – This was a really bad idea for yet another Mad Max film filled with yelling, screaming, sand, and junked up cars. Except for the sand, it could have been filmed in New York City during rush hour, but that's just my opinion. A waste of Charlize Theron!

The Streak

My streak is over. It was a streak that lasted 30 years and one I was kind of proud of, but it is over. It began in 1986 on the White House lawn as President Reagan flew off to Reykjavik, Iceland, to meet then President Gorbachev of the Soviet Union for discussions about intermediate nuclear missiles. My friend Jim had a connection who got us tickets to be on the lawn that day and to watch the President depart on Marine One (the official Presidential Helicopter). Jim and I stood there in the large crowd, and I remember looking down for a few moments when suddenly Jim was gone. The crowd had jostled us a bit and suddenly we were yards apart. As the President was walking towards the helicopter, he paused to shake hands with some folks he knew and before I knew it, there I was, in front of the President shaking his hand. I was accidentally in the right place at the right time.

That was the first time I met the President of the United States. I will admit that my definition of meeting is simply shaking his hand and/or having a short conversation with him. That streak continued up to President Obama. It stopped when Trump was elected. I have never met Trump, and I have no plans to ever meet him and feel just fine about that.

Here is a short recap of those meetings:

- I met George Bush while working in the U.S. Senate while he was still Vice President. I will admit he wasn't President yet, but I met him in the Republican Cloak Room and I am counting it. It was a very short hello and a quick handshake but it meets my definition.
- I met Bill Clinton at a Democratic fundraiser that takes place in Northern Virginia every year called the Kennedy King Dinner. He was leaving the stage and I shook his hand. I also met Hillary at another of these events but, well, hey that did not come to pass and that leads us back to Trump, and so let's just move on.
- That takes us to George W. Bush. At the time that Bush was President, I was serving as a school board member in Fairfax County. Bush appeared at one of our schools in Fairfax to make

some education related policy speech. I was lucky enough, given my meager political position, to be in the second row of the auditorium. Seated in front of me was one of our U.S. senators from Virginia. He leaned back and whispered to me that the President will exit the stage to our left and will shake hands with folks in the front row. The senator invited me up next to him as soon as the speech ended. I met the President and chatted with him for about a minute.

- Some years later, I met President Obama. He was running for the presidency at the time (2007) and was also visiting one of our schools in Fairfax. After his speech, I was able to meet him and shake hands.

That's the streak, and now it's over. Since I have no plans to meet Trump, I will see about kicking off a new streak after he is gone. Any bets on who it will be?

The Master Politician

It is 1994, and I am attending the Kennedy King Dinner in Alexandria, Virginia. I am in a large ballroom, and on the stage, sit about 15 local politicians and the President of the United States, Bill Clinton. Clinton is seated center stage. The program is structured in such a way that the President does not speak first, he is scheduled to speak last. Clinton sits there quietly with a calm expression on his face. The others talk, and talk, and talk. Each speaker, from local county supervisors up to congressmen and the governor, relish their opportunity to be on stage with the President and so they do go on. Nobody pays them much attention – we are all waiting for the main event. Clinton sits patiently. He looks relaxed, as if he is dreaming about sitting on a tropical island with not a care in the world. It's a façade.

The speakers drone on as we all wait for the President to speak. Finally, it is time for the President. He walks to the podium, but rather than go into his prepared remarks, he modifies his remarks. He has not been daydreaming about an island in the Pacific, he has been listening intently. He incorporates snippets from the remarks of then Governor Doug Wilder, Senator Chuck Robb, and many others into his speech. He sat there, taking mental notes, identifying the key issues, and personalities, and weaves a story based on what he has heard. I am impressed and mesmerized.

It is a brilliant display. I am astonished at the respect he has shown to all the speakers that preceded him. I wonder if I could have done such a thing. I doubt it. I actually enjoy public speaking, but this is beyond my skills. The man is a master politician and this is meant as a true compliment.

A Revised Bill of Rights

I listen with amusement to all the TV commentators talking about our Founding Fathers as if they were this homogenous collective of men who agreed on everything. They did not. They argued intensely about our Constitution and the Bill of Rights. In fact, so many commentators focus on the Federalists (e.g., Madison and Hamilton) that they forget about the Anti-Federalists (George Mason, Patrick Henry, and others) and how they helped to ensure the Bill of Rights was part and parcel of what was enacted in 1791.

Now don't get me wrong, the Bill of Rights is a fine document, but as I get older, I wonder if we might consider making some adjustments – just for fun. As I write this little essay, I am 56 years old. (Where the heck did the years go? I have no idea.) As I said, I am 56 but you get no prize for turning 56. Remember back when you were 16 and you got to drive on or around your birthday. Yes, you had to pass a test and earn that privilege but first you had to reach 16 years of age. Then, at 18, you could vote. Then, at 21, you could drink. But what happens after that? I will tell you what – nothing, nada. You get "bupkis." After you hit 21, you don't gain any additional privileges, you just add grey hair. No more rewards, no more privileges, just more birthdays. I say this must end!

I say it is time to change all that. And this leads us inexorably back to the Bill of Rights, believe it or not. The rights bestowed upon us in the Bill of Rights are applied equally to us all – or at least they should be. But here is my weird, but brilliant idea. Let's now bestow these rights over time as we grow older. What type of heresy is this you say? Give me a moment to explain.

Let's begin by considering the Fourth Amendment which prevents unreasonable search and seizure. I say you don't get that one until you are 25. As a parent, I still want to be able to check on my kids – especially if they are still living under my roof! So now at 25, you can celebrate the right of privacy from your parents.

Now let's tackle the big one – the First Amendment, which gives you the right to free speech among other things. Well, personally (and probably because I am 56), I would rather you just keep your mouth shut until you're about 30. At 30, I believe you may have gained enough wisdom, experience, and knowledge to have something worthy to say. But basically, until you're 30, just shut the fuck up, or talk amongst yourselves – either way I don't want to hear how smart and worldly you are when you are clearly neither. So, happy birthday to all 30-year olds, you now have freedom of speech! The First Amendment also gives us the right to peaceably assemble. Let's say we grant that particular right to those reaching the ripe old age of 35. That sounds about right. Isn't this fun? (I realize I have probably alienated anyone younger than 40 here but heck, they don't read books anymore anyway.)

As most of us know, the Second Amendment gives us the right to bear arms. Specifically, it says "A well-regulated militia being necessary to the security of a free state, the right of the people to keep and bear arms shall not be infringed." We can debate what that exactly means, and for those interested, there was a great article written by former Associate Supreme Court Justice John Paul Stevens in the *Washington Post* in April of 2014 – look it up.

Now this is just me talking but if truth be told, I would be a much happier camper if you could not purchase a gun until you were 40 years old. So, moving forward, you get to be 40 and you can purchase a gun. Congrats to all you 40-year old's.

Obviously (at least I hope it's obvious), I am just having some fun here and the above should not be taken seriously, unless of course you agree with me. If that is the case, you are almost definitely over 40 and you can help me develop appropriate ages for the remaining rights listed in the Bill of Rights. Together we can make history!

Space – The Final Frontier

On March 7, 2009 NASA launched the Kepler space observatory. The observatory was named after astronomer Johannes Kepler, a good friend of mine back in the day (assuming that day was around 1600 and you believe in reincarnation).

The observatory's mission was to explore strange new worlds, to seek out new life and new civilizations, to boldly go where no man has gone before. Oh, sorry I got carried away there; but in reality, Kepler was designed to discover Earth-size planets orbiting other stars, so kind of Star Trek like.

Anyway, NASA allowed any individual to include a personal message on the Kepler observatory. I can't recall if the messages were inscribed on the observatory or were recorded in some digital fashion. Anyway, I sent the following message out on the Kepler Probe. Since I am not likely to ever get into space, this message is about the best I can do.

"Are we alone in the universe? Certain questions are eternal and possess their own inherent significance. Finding out our place in the universe is a question whose importance cannot be understated.

This mission seeks to help mankind unravel that mystery and for that reason alone merits our attention, our respect, and our prayers and good wishes.

While we as yet can journey no further than our own planetary neighborhood this mission will reach out into the abyss and with it, these words and others that demonstrate our desire to find our place in the universe and perhaps find others like us."

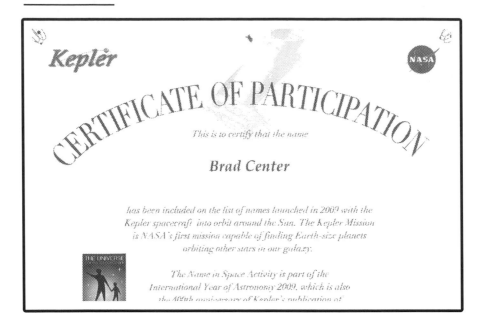

Here is the certificate I received from NASA.

In 2016, I again got to vicariously reach the stars. I was in San Antonio for a business meeting. The company I worked for at the time invited a former astronaut Col. Chris Hadfield to be our guest speaker. Col. Hadfield commanded the Space Station and several shuttle flights. I listened to him speak, and his stories were fascinating. He told us that when you get into the shuttle on launch day, you run through all your checks and do everything possible to make the mission a success but in the end, you know that at the end of the day you will either be in space above the earth or you will be dead. That statement brings home the reality of just what these men and women must deal with as astronauts. As I said, I may never get into space myself but meeting an astronaut was something very special indeed.

A picture of me and astronaut Chris Hadfield.

A Wedding Foreshadowed

I got married at 27. I met my soon-to-be wife at a party in Washington D.C. about two years before. Her name was Melanie. Now, I know what you are thinking, you said you married Valerie. Just who the heck is Melanie? I will explain, and I did indeed marry Valerie; I just didn't say I married her right away – we will get there.

I met Melanie and we dated for some time, eventually moving in together. Looking back on the relationship now, we made better friends than husband and wife, but it is always easier to be smarter later. Anyway, Melanie approached me a few months before the wedding and told me she wanted her good friend (let's call him Leif, as in Leif Erickson of Viking fame – that is obviously not his name but I like using historical names) Leif in the wedding party. I had no real objections to having Leif as one of my groomsmen but that meant we needed to add a bridesmaid to Melanie's side to even things out.

I told Melanie that I thought a trade was in order. I told her that I would take Leif as one of my groomsmen if she added my good friend Valerie to her side. I also suggested that I get two first-round draft choices but Melanie didn't get the joke, she was not big into sports. Melanie pondered it and agreed to this slightly odd concept – and that, my friends, is how Valerie, my one-day wife, not only attended my first wedding, but was actually in my wedding.

As you may recall, I told you how Val and I met back in 12th grade. While I fell in love with her almost immediately, it took her just a bit longer – say around 10 years or so. In the time between, she married a nice man and lived outside of Philadelphia, and I went off to graduate school in Washington D.C. Deep in the back of mind, I still loved her, but I had done my best to bury that feeling because I had resigned myself that it just was not to be. We stayed in touch during that time and remained close friends.

The wedding to Melanie was a nice affair and all my good friends were there, to include Rich Kosoff, who actually escorted Val down the aisle. I recall looking back and seeing Val come down the aisle, it was just the oddest feeling, marrying Melanie and at the same time seeing Val walk down that aisle. I cared deeply about Melanie but this was truly a surreal experience.

My marriage to Melanie did not last very long and we divorced amicably. Love doesn't always last. Val and her husband did the same about a year after Melanie and I divorced. You can probably see where that will lead. Three years later I walked down the aisle with Val on my arm.

Two related notes to my marriage ceremony with Melanie:

Note 1: A few days before the marriage, both Richard and Val arrived in D.C. for the wedding and I took them for a short tour of the city. They were trouble-makers the whole time! They were having the greatest time, screwing with me as we toured the Capitol. They tried to sneak into the elevator reserved for senators only, they sat on Senator Spector's desk (the whole office was empty but still!), they even tried to sit in the part of the tram reserved for senators, and I have already relayed how much of a big deal that is. I was way too serious about that kind of stuff back then, and they had a great deal of fun at my expense.

Note 2: Attending the wedding were Leif and his girlfriend and soon to be wife who we will refer to as Carmela (also not her real name). Also in attendance at the wedding was a woman I worked with while I was at the Inspector General's Office for the DoD. We will refer to her as Sabrina. All of these folks will show up again in a later story, so I wanted to introduce them now. Please keep your scorecard handy as you can't tell the players without your scorecard. It is going to get interesting.

Mustard Gas and Arkansas – A Great Combination

In my late 20s, I worked for the Army Inspector General's Office. In the job, I got to travel to some fascinating places and see some very interesting things. Pine Bluff, Arkansas was not among those fascinating places, but there is a tale to be told about my trip there.

Pine Bluff, Arkansas is a "one-horse town." In this case, the horse in question was the Pine Bluff Arsenal, operated by the U.S. Army. Besides that, Pine Bluff had a rundown mall and not much else to speak of – sorry Pine Bluff.

I was in Pine Bluff with my team to do an inspection of how the arsenal handled their hazardous waste and materials and Pine Bluff Arsenal had a lot of that. One of the duties of the arsenal was the storage and decommissioning of various chemical weapons such as Mustard Gas and BZ (a psycho-chemical agent) – basically nasty shit. To properly work and/or tour the facility, you needed to have a gas mask with you at all times, just in case there was an accident at the facility. I was given a gas mask, but it had to be properly fitted for each person. Keep in mind, I had never been in the military, so all of this was extremely new to me and kind of surreal – here I was getting fitted for a gas mask.

Here is how it worked. They select a mask for you and then show you how to tighten it so fumes cannot get in. To make sure the fit is secure, they bring you into a special chamber where you put on the mask and they pump in a very strong-smelling gas that smells like a truckload of bananas. If the mask has been fitted properly you won't smell a thing. As part of the test, they have you crack the seal on the mask for just a second and then the smell of bananas comes pouring in.

I kept that mask on my hip for a full week as we conducted our inspection of the arsenal. Fortunately, it never left my hip. I suspect that property values in Pine Bluff are very cheap, and I also wonder if they throw in a complimentary gas mask during settlement.

Things I Hate, Shortcomings, Rules and other Miscellaneous Stuff

Nobody's perfect, certainly not me. As such, there are some things that I just hate or generally suck at. In most cases, they amount to the same thing. Let me begin with my total ineptitude at anything that requires what I refer to as the "handy gene." In other words, I have no ability to fix, build, or otherwise do anything around the house or with a car. I realize, I lose some points in the "manly" category, but seriously I just suck at this stuff. Ask me to lift something, ask me to smash something, ask me to do anything that requires brute strength, and I am fine but ask me to do anything that requires any actual skill or talent in this area, and I am a total washout. Hence, I hate to do any of it. My wife doesn't especially love doing these things either, but she will persevere and get it done if the need arises. She even takes some satisfaction in completing the job. Not I. My first response is, why we don't we hire someone to do whatever problem arises.

In a somewhat similar vein, while I have some talents in athletic world, skiing is not one of these. I have tried this "pastime of Beelzebub" (as I refer to it) a couple of times and I just stink. But the fun doesn't stop there; no – when you are attempting to ski, you have to add the cold, the continuous pain from falling, and the sheer embarrassment of watching 5-year-olds pass you on the bunny slope. I don't get it and hope I never again put on a pair of skis.

I also must also confess to a pure hatred of lines. I hate to wait in line. Now, I know I am not alone in this, but my hatred of lines is staggering. Let me put it this way: If there is a physical heaven and for some unknown reason, I am headed in that direction (hard to believe), and there is a line to get into said heaven, I am not waiting. I will give it 30 minutes max. If it takes longer than that to get into heaven, I will simply go to hell! I wonder if you can get a Fast Pass for heaven? Seriously, someone at Disney should look into that.

Speaking of wasting time, cooking, to me, is a complete waste of time. Yes, I know how delicious food can be, I am not an idiot. But I just don't get spending hours cooking a meal that takes ten minutes to eat! What a waste! This is why God invented restaurants and take-out food. Right? My rule is simple, if it takes longer to cook than it does to eat, it is not worth it!

While we are on the subject of food, I have two rules about food that guide me. Rule 1: I will not eat anything that is cute. For example, I won't eat a deer. Bambi is cute. The same goes for rabbits, lambs, and other generally furry creatures. I have no issues with cows, pigs, turkeys, chickens, because they just don't pass the cute threshold. Rule 2 is also important: never eat an animal that you named. So, if you are living on a farm and there is a pig on the farm, you can go ahead and eat it when the time is right but if you (at any point) give that pig a name, then you just can't eat it. The pig may not be cute, but now it has a name and you just can't eat it.

Now that we are on the subject of rules, I have my own rule related to sports. In order for what you are doing to be considered a sport, you need to have two things:

- First, you need a ball. If there isn't ball, it is not a sport – sorry hockey fans, get a ball.
- Second, a sport must be timed. If there isn't a time element to the activity, then it is not a sport.

Basketball, football, tennis, baseball, rugby, even water polo are all sports. Cycling, boxing, figure skating, gymnastics are not sports – sorry, this is not personal, it is just the way that it is. Additionally, while I love golf, it also doesn't qualify as a true sport. It has a ball and is timed in a loose fashion, but basically any sport you can perform while drinking a beer is more of a pastime (also true for bowling). That doesn't mean that activities like figure skating or gymnastics are easy things to do but they just aren't a sport. So sayeth Brad Center – for no rational reason whatsoever, except I am generally much better at things that have a ball.

One last rule of mine: don't let me catch you eating pizza with a knife and fork! That's just wrong. That's it I'm done with my rules. However, there is a list of rules I once read, which I am happy to impart:

1. Never play cards with a guy name Doc
2. Never eat in a place called Mom's
3. Never go to bed with a woman whose problems are worse than your own (apply any sexual paring that applies to you for that one, the point is the same)
4. And never under any circumstances let anyone catch you puking your guts out over the toilet, especially a woman whose problems are worse than your own.

By the way breaking Rule 3 is a huge mistake – trust me!

The Intermediate-Range Nuclear Forces Treaty

I am 27 years old and I am working on Capitol Hill for Senator Specter, as you may remember. In fact, I just turned 27 a month before, and now I am standing on the Senate floor about to introduce an amendment to a treaty involving nuclear weapons. Well to be honest, I am about to introduce two amendments being offered by Senator Arlen Specter to the treaty.

Let me backtrack just a moment and tell you that Specter had just called me and his Legislative Assistant (Harry) to the Senate floor. We arrive on the floor of the Senate, and Specter beckons us over to him. Specter tells us that he has two amendments he would like to make. He tells Harry and I that he knows they are not likely to pass but he has a point he wants to make. So, Specter rattles off the amendments to us really fast, and Harry and I do our best to write down exactly what he is saying. He finishes and waits for us to raise our heads from our transcription. We look at Specter and he asks us if we got it. Harry says, "yes." We start to head up to the clerk to submit the amendments when I pause and turn. Specter says, "Brad, do you have a question?"

"Senator," I say, "This is important, and I just want to make sure I got this exactly the way you want." I read back the language and he nods. "Okay, got it," I say.

I turn and Harry is looking at me like I had just done something horrific. I tell him, "Look, you may think you had it, but I am not fucking this up. Better to be safe and risk getting Specter mad now then having him flip if we blow this." Harry begrudgingly nods, and we give the amendments to the clerk. They are defeated as Specter predicts, but at least they are accurate.

The debate continues for another hour, but the treaty is not passed that day. Senators begin to filter out of the Chamber. Specter is seated at his desk and asks me to sit next to him. I sit down in the desk next to Specter. We talk about the day and he asks me, "Brad, what do you want to do in the future?" I look at him for a moment. I meet his gaze and tell him that

I want to sit right here someday at my own desk. He smiles. I think he likes my chutzpah.

The next day arrives and the Senators are still debating the treaty. Senators come and go in the Chamber as they usually do throughout the day. As the day draws to a close, Senator Byrd and Senator Dole, who are the majority and minority leaders in the Senate, call all the senators to the Chamber. They are all seated at their desks! I am in the back of the Chamber watching. This almost never happens; they are all seated in their desks waiting. Byrd and Dole begin to lecture the group. They tell them that we are passing this darn treaty tomorrow – end of discussion. I look at the scene and suddenly the power of the Senate is omnipresent. They are all here. They are all seated and at attention. The power in the air is almost palpable. I am a bit in awe.

The next day, that treaty is ratified almost unanimously.

Coming Full Circle

Sit back and relax. Find a comfortable chair. You may even want to actually turn off your phone! Really! This is a good one.

So, you will recall that my marriage to Melanie did not last very long, and Melanie moved out of our apartment. I will add, that it was Melanie's idea to break up. I will also add that I was pretty broken up about this at the time. Having said all that, it ended up being the right thing for everyone but in the moment, it hurt like lying on a bed of nails, dipped in acid.

After the pain subsided, I walked around in a fugue state for some time. I existed, but didn't feel much of anything. I went through the motions of daily life, but wasn't really alive. As time wore on, I awoke from my fugue and found that the world was still there. I am just not built to sit idly by, so I pushed myself back into the world, gently at first, like tasting a new food for the first time. I sniffed life, then nibbled it, and rolled it around on my tongue before I swallowed. At first, it didn't taste like much, and I was happy that it simply didn't burn or taste sour. As I continued to nibble at life's offerings, slowly I began to taste all the flavors of life once again, and I found out how hungry I actually was.

At about the same time that Melanie and I split, Leif (who I introduced to you before) broke up with his wife Carmella. So, in true sitcom fashion, Leif moved in with me, and Carmella moved in with Melanie. However, life isn't a sitcom, and so I **_will not_** be sharing the hijinks and laughs that ensued as these two crazy couples continually found opportunities for miscommunication and laughter. Life is not a '70s style sitcom. Nope, that never happened. However, what did happen is a tale worth telling.

Leif moved in as my roommate. We talked and generally got along, but we were not close. Besides, I was traveling a lot for work and didn't have too much free time. The free time I did have, I spent getting back into the wonderful world of dating. I was single again, what else was I going to do? The funny thing about the time between my divorce from Melanie and getting together with Valerie was how odd the dating scene was for me.

I went on a date, and sometimes it ended with a polite kiss on the check and other times, well, let's simply say it went much further. I could never seem to tell how it was going to go. I just went with the flow.

One girl I went out with during that time was a nice young girl named Sabrina, who I had met while I was working for the federal government. I dated Sabrina for a while but as I said, I was travelling and while we had some good times, the relationship eventually started to fade. Of course, the fact that my good roommate Leif decided to make a move on Sabrina during my travels may have exacerbated the end of that relationship! As I said, Sabrina and I were trailing off a bit, so I was not heartbroken but it was bad form on Leif's part. You just don't do that to a roommate – it's in the freaking roommate code! Needless to say, Leif and I did not speak much after that.

Enter Valerie. After my divorce, I reached out to Val and she was a good friend during that period. We didn't see each other much, but I called often enough and she was a comforting voice. As time passed two things happened.

First, Val and her husband decided to get a divorce. They had been married about five years, but Valerie just didn't feel fulfilled in the marriage and she knew she had to end things if she was ever going to find what she was ultimately looking for – oddly enough that was me. When Val told me about her separation from her husband, I was not sure how to feel. On the one hand, you are never happy to hear about this type of thing, and I had just experienced that type of pain first-hand. But on the other hand, this was "The Girl." In the back of my mind, I had always considered Val as "the one." Now I could let that feeling begin to take shape in my mind and in my heart and pursue what I always wanted.

The second thing that happened was that Sabrina and Leif grew closer and closer. Eventually Leif and Sabrina moved into together and became engaged. So, my former roommate and girlfriend were engaged – how odd. But, then again, I was now dating Val who was one of my oldest friends and who had been in my wedding party to Melanie, so strange is a relative thing. In fact, Val eventually moved down to Virginia to be with me and we moved in together.

So, let's pause now and review the bidding:

- Brad marries Melanie.
- Brad and Melanie split.
- Melanie moves in with Carmela.
- Leif moves in with Brad.
- Brad and Sabrina date and then fade.
- Leif starts dating Sabrina.
- Val and her husband split up.
- Brad and Valerie begin to date.
- Val moves to Virginia and moves in with Brad.
- Leif and Sabrina get engaged and move in together.

Ok, now that we are all up to speed. Let's move on to ***The Party*** and the ultimate reason for this story. Leif and Sabrina throw a party. It may have been an engagement party or it may have been some other celebration, but in any event, we received an invitation to come to their apartment for the celebration. I asked Val how she felt about going and she said that we should go. I said OK, not knowing what to expect. It turns out that there were about 20 people attending, stuffed into a small apartment in Alexandria, Virginia, and the events, for me, got a little weird.

Now it turns out that Melanie (being a good friend of Leif's) was also invited. At some point during the evening I found myself in a small living room and seated to my left was Valerie, seated to my immediate right was Melanie, and seated diagonally across from me was Sabrina. Suddenly, I am struck with an odd thought – there are about five or six women in the room at that moment, and I have slept with three of them! Now let's be clear here; my name is Brad Center, not Brad Pitt and so the odds of something like this happening are pretty darn slim. It's almost the equivalent of the Beatles getting back together and that seems like long odds since two of the "Fab Four" (John Lennon and George Harrison) are dead.

As the shock wore off, I looked around the room and turned to Val. She seemed to understand the situation. I smiled at her. What else could I do? We were together, we were happy, the rest was just background noise. Well that's the story. I took you all the way through this soap opera to get you to this party and the odd circumstance of being in a room with three women I had been intimate with. Life is strange – maybe it is a sitcom after all.

I am an Elitist Snob

I may not be a bumpkin, but I can be an elitist snob sometimes, well, maybe most of the time. OK, maybe all the time. Let me explain. Never mind, there is no explanation, I have a character flaw, and I own it. I will say that my snobbery is focused to a select number of items – books, music, and general knowledge (history, science). Of course, that pretty much covers everything, so we are back once again to me being a total snob. To give you a glimpse into this character flaw, let me provide the following little tidbit.

I was introduced to a very nice girl at a party while in graduate school. We talked and hit it off fairly well. I asked her out, and we had a couple of dates. These went well enough, and one evening, she asked me if I wanted to come over to her place after dinner. I said great, figuring one thing might likely lead to another. I was in my 20s and a big fan of "one thing leading to another." I got to her apartment. It was an efficiency apartment, so basically as soon as you walked in you were in the bedroom/living room. She said she was going to go to the bathroom and to make myself at home.

I stared at the apartment. My eyes found her bookcase. I scanned through the titles, while she performed whatever women do in the bathroom in situations like this. In her bookcase, I found a bunch of Danielle Steel titles. Inside my head, the elitist snob shouted, "Check please!" I did not care if she stepped out of the bathroom wearing nothing at all, I was not going to bed with a Danielle Steel fan. She did not come out naked, but I think things would have progressed nicely had I been so inclined. But, not tonight and not for me. I made up some excuse about being tired or something and left. I called a few days later and told her that I didn't think we were a good match. I am sure she agreed.

I will submit one additional piece of evidence in my own self-prosecution, and here it is. I don't care what you believe as long as you understand what you believe. For example, I don't care if you call yourself a Jew, Christian, Muslim, Seventh Day Adventist, Jehovah's Witness, whatever, it makes no difference to me. But, if you say you that you're a Christian (as an example) then you should understand what that means. You should understand the basic tenants of Christianity. I have seen way too many people who have no clue what their religion actually says and yet say they are a believer. That drives me crazy. The same goes for political beliefs – again, I don't care which side of the political spectrum you fall, but if you proudly call yourself a Democrat or a Republican or some other affiliation, know what that party stands for. To me, you sound like an idiot if you can't articulate what your group stands for. I just have no patience or tolerance for that type of ignorance.

There you have it; I am an elitist snob – I own it.

And Speaking of Books

Has an author or a book ever altered you profoundly? I would argue that if you cannot point to some book or some author that has made its mark on your life, has not molded your soul, or has not made you look anew at your notions of reality and the human condition, then you have cheated yourself out of something very special. I love the written word and what a great author can do to your heart and mind by simply putting these little phonetic symbols upon paper.

Personally, I cannot point to a single book or a single author that is my ultimate favorite – pitting one author against another just doesn't make that much sense to me and here's why. When I read a novel, I look at four specific things.

The first thing I look for are interesting characters that I care about as a reader. Does the author then develop these characters to the point that I understand their actions and motives? There have been, and continue to be, many great authors who develop memorable characters – characters who even take on a life of their own outside the confines of the novel where they were born. One of my favorite authors in this category is John Irving. His works are full of memorable and quirky characters -- Owen Meany, Garp, and Ruth Cole (*A Widow for One Year*) come instantly to mind.

The second thing I look for is a great plot to drive the story along. One reason I respect an author who can develop an interesting and yet plausible plot line is that I struggle mightily with this aspect of writing. I am constantly amazed at a good writer's ability to think ten moves ahead, like a master chess champion. Each character, like a piece on the chess board, is played and pitted against one another at the right time. This is even more impressive when you remember that (in a sense) the writer is playing both sides of the chess board. So, whether you're talking about a master of horror like Stephen King, or a master of suspense like Grisham, le Carré, Dan Brown, or Michael Crichton (name your favorite), they all can take you a journey far from the ordinary to a place that logic somewhat defies but where the heart wants to travel.

The third important element in any great book is having something to say. What I mean by that, is that the author should have a point of view.

He or she should try to impart some insight into the human condition or put forth some interesting knowledge. I want to learn something new or find a new way of looking at things. I want to be challenged. Preferably, I would like to come to a "Major Knowing" (thank you Richard Bach). For me, there is no better genre for this than science/speculative fiction. Science/Speculative fiction, when done well, enables the writer to provide a unique perspective on our society, culture, and history as the ultimate outsider looking in. Again, when it is done well, you can learn so much.

As you already know, Ellison is one of my favorites but there are tons of others from Orwell and Burgess to more modern authors like Nancy Kress and William Gibson. But, there are literally dozens of great authors in this genre such as Lester Del Ray, Daniel Keys, Phillip K Dick, Arthur C. Clarke, Orson Scott Card, Ursula K. Le Guin, Kim Stanley Robinson, Spider Robinson, or Greg Egan. The list goes on and on. I should add a special nod to authors who defy categorization and flip reality on its head. They give us a look at the world from a totally different perspective. Authors like Vonnegut and James Morrow come to mind.

Last, but not least, is the author's ability to manipulate language and create from a simple set of words some imagery or some linguistic feat that causes you pause amid reading and say:

- "God, I wish I had written that."
- "What an incredibly cleaver turn of phrase."
- "How the hell did he come up with that?"
- "All the good words have been taken – I think I will lay down my pen."

I know I've uttered these and other phrases when I come across an author who knows how to use the written word. One of my favorites is Tom Robbins. He has an incredible ability to use language in interesting and unique ways. He's quirky, contemporary, and ridiculously whimsical. He creates a vibrant picture with words, dabbing color here and there to create a masterpiece of written expression. Unfortunately, I am no Tom Robbins and my description does not do him justice. Read something of his, I promise it will be worth it.

As I said, I don't think I can pin down just one author or one book but here are some strong science/speculative fiction stories to consider:

1. "I Have No Mouth and I Must Scream" – Harlan Ellison (see the following story)
2. "The Part of Us That Loves" – Kim Stanley Robinson
3. "In Spirit" – Pat Forde
4. "God is an Iron" – Spider Robinson
5. "Deathbird" – Harlan Ellison
6. "Learning to Be Me" – Greg Egan
7. "Arties Angels" – Catherine Wells
8. "Evensong" – Lester Del Ray
9. "Silver" – Steven Spruill
10. "Beggars in Spain" – Nancy Kress
11. "Paingod" – Harlan Ellison
12. "Schrodinger's Kitten" – George Alec Effinger
13. "The Last Question" – Issac Asimov
14. "Spelling God with the Wrong Blocks" – James Morrow
15. "Delusions For a Dragon Slayer"– Harlan Ellison
16. "The Deluge" – James Morrow
17. "Basilisk" – Harlan Ellison
18. "Goodnight Moon" – Annie Bellet
19. "'Repent, Harlequin!' Said the Ticktock Man" – Harlan Ellison
20. "Diary of a Mad Deity" – James Morrow
21. "Grail" – Harlan Ellison
22. "Dear John" – Robin Wasserman
23. "The Star" – Arthur C. Clarke
24. "The Cold Equations" – Tom Godwin

My last word on writing deals with "Finnegan's Wake." Can someone please explain this book to me? I have tried to read it – really, I have! I get a few pages into it and feel as if I have stumbled into an alternate reality and I have no context for anything I am reading. I think either I am missing something or it is the biggest literary joke ever played.

I Have Two Hands and I Must Applaud

It is 1995, I am about to meet someone whose work I greatly admire. I am on way to Old Town Alexandria where Harlan Ellison is holding a book signing event outside a local bookstore (back in the day where there were actual local bookstores or bookstores at all). My friend Mike and I park and get a place in line. There are all sorts of people here, from all walks of life it appears to me. There are at least 200 people in a line all the way down the block. We wait, as we eventually draw closer.

Harlan Ellison is a prolific author of speculative fiction. He detests the term *science fiction* but the term can be used as a general pointer to those not acquainted with Ellison and the type of fiction he writes. But Harlan is right, his work is not truly science fiction. There are no spaceships going warp speed, no aliens trying to conquer the planet, and no one from the future who travels back in time. Rather, he twists reality just a bit to suit his storylines and presents the reader with compelling short stories that make you think and challenge your perspective.

In addition to being a first-class storyteller, Harlan Ellison has a reputation of being extremely opinionated and off-putting to some. We eventually get close enough to hear Harlan engage with his fans. He is seated outside the store, and it is a beautiful afternoon. I listen the exchanges. He is telling jokes, laughing with the fans. I had worried, given his reputation, what he would be like with his fans. Would he be patronizing or would he be appreciative? I am relieved to see that he appears as happy as I am to be here.

In front of me is a young man dressed in a suit and tie. To be perfectly honest, he is a tad nerdy looking. He stands in front of Ellison and starts to speak. His words come out slowly at first in a hushed voice, almost a whisper, and then they pour forth quickly as if he has only a certain amount of time left to speak before he dies. He tells Ellison how much his work has meant to him. He tells him how much he admires him. He tells him how much he has changed his life. I tense. Here it comes, Ellison will pity him and tell him to get a life. He will berate him for living his life in books or some other mean-spirited remark. I am wrong – completely and utterly wrong. Harlan thanks him profusely and turns to crowd and tells us that his fans come in all shapes and sizes – from bankers to bikers.

Now it is my turn. I hand Harlan my copy of "Alone Against Tomorrow." He signs it and then turns to the introduction to a story called "Are You Listening?" and begins to cross out some text.

I look down at Harlan and ask, "What are you doing there?"

He looks up and says, "Who wrote the book?"

Sheepishly I say, "Well you did."

He smiles, "That's right, so if you don't mind, I have just a few updates to make." I smile back and tell him to go right ahead.

My copy now has some unique changes and the following notation at the front of the book: "Altered By Author's Hand 9, April, 95." I am just fine with that.

Musical Interlude #1

I love music, but God has cursed me with absolute no musical talent. I cannot for the life of me play an instrument. Reading music is no easier to me than understanding Latin. And just to top it off, I have a poor singing voice. I have the ability to hold a note for no more than a millisecond. Sometimes, in the car, I will be singing along to a piece of music, and I must stop because I am so far off-key, that it hurts my own sensibilities. It's embarrassing.

But I love music. In particular, I love classic rock, which is natural enough given that I grew up in the late '60s and '70s. As I write this, I have my iPhone next to the computer and "Karn Evil 9: 1st Impression, Part 2" is playing (Emerson, Lake and Palmer). I have no story to tell here, but didn't think I could write this book without a nod to my favorite progressive rock bands Kansas and Alan Parsons. I love a ton of other bands but these two stand out for me. They are not everyone's favorites but they are mine – no apologies.

Musical Interlude #2

Has there ever been a line from a song that just drove deep into your heart, so deep that it felt seared into the very fabric of your being? I can think of few that have hit me that hard. As I write, two jump out at me.

There is a song by Simon & Garfunkel simply called "America." A young couple is traveling the country by bus and in the middle of the song they sing –

"Kathy, I'm lost," I said, though I knew she was sleeping

I'm empty and aching and I don't know why

Simple lyrics but they crush me every time I hear them. The pain radiates across me, though me, and around me. I am drowning in an abyss of sorrow just from that short phrase. I don't know why it impacts me so, and I have never mentioned this before to anyone. There you have it.

Joan Baez wrote a song back in the day called "Diamonds and Rust." There have been various covers of the song by various artists, but I happen to like the original and the version done by Blackmore's Night. There is a verse in the song that goes like this:

Now I see you standing with brown leaves all around and snow in your hair

Now you're smiling out the window of that crummy hotel over Washington Square

Our breath comes in white clouds, mingles and hangs in the air

Speaking strictly for me we both could've died then and there

At first blush that might not seem like an affirmation of life and love, but to me it is. It also speaks to me a of a perfect moment where the universe has presented itself fully, and you wish that you could hold that perfect moment forever and never leave it. But time moves on, as it must, and so we continue on, but if you could choose a perfect moment in which to freeze your life and enter eternity, this one moment would be the one – it is that special.

Those are just two, there are others but I will let you fill the pages of your book with your own choices.

Remember the Alamo

The sole purpose of this little story to brag about how romantic I am! No, strike that. It is to tell you how romantic I can be when it comes to my wife. Yes, that is much better. I am probably still in trouble for the first sentence, but the second one is probably closer to the truth.

Val and I had been together for about a year and I thought it was time to propose and start our lives together "officially." Val had to go down to San Antonio for a conference, so I started my planning. I would fly down a day or so after she left and surprise her. I called the hotel and told them to give her a note, telling her, "An old friend wishes to meet you at the Stetson's Restaurant to answer the age-old question, "Who will take care of me?"

Val got the note but wasn't sure if I was actually going to show in person or arrange something else – perhaps send some flowers or something when she got to the restaurant. Our bank account wasn't exactly flush with cash back then, and so she just wasn't sure what I had planned.

Well, I got there and met her at Stetson's. It was a beautiful night on the Riverwalk and I popped the question. She said yes, what else could she do? I just spent the last of our money flying down there and it would be a pity if I had wasted all that money. In truth, we were both excited and ready to get married.

Now, I must admit that Val's excellent scrapbooking skills helped with this story because if the truth be told, I had no idea (some 26 years later) the name of the restaurant in San Antonio, but there it was in the scrapbook.

One Hot Affair

It was July 20, 1991 and 101 degrees outside. A beautiful day for a wedding if you are a camel or a lizard. But let's rewind just a bit before the solar flare that was to be my wedding to Val.

We had gotten engaged and started planning for the wedding some months before. We were both on our second wedding and wanted to manage this one ourselves. First, we needed to pick a location. Many in our families live in and around Philadelphia but we also have friends in the Virginia, D.C., and Maryland area. In addition to picking a centralized location or at least sort of central (we leaned towards the family in Philly), we wanted an interesting place to hold the wedding. We found a great location: the Duportail House near Valley Forge, PA. Duportail is a French name and is pronounced "Du-Por-Tie." The house dates to revolutionary times, and while upgrades and additions have been made, it is still an older style building. The house has charm and we booked it for our wedding.

We also needed someone to perform the ceremony. Val is a Methodist, and I was born and raised Jewish, so we had to find something that would work. We found the perfect person in Gordon Hutchins who was a retired Army Chaplin. We spoke to him, and he had no trouble putting together a non-denominational, yet spiritual, service for us.

It was the day before the wedding, and Val and I decided to do something goofy. We got my brother and a good friend of Val's together, and we went miniature golfing in Northeast Philly on Roosevelt Boulevard. I grew up playing on that miniature golf course, so it was nostalgic and goofy at the same time. The golf course was a classic miniature golf course with each hole themed with some animal sculpture – total kitsch. The 18th hole had a seal that had a ball spinning on its nose. The ball was red and white striped, and to win a free game, you had to hit the ball up a ramp and into a slot in the ball. That miniature golf course is no longer there but I have fond memories.

The day of the miniature golf was hot, but not as hot as it got on the wedding day. As I said, it peaked that day at 101 degrees. To make things a bit less stressful, we booked a couple of rooms at a nearby hotel for us to change before the wedding. Val and I had one room, and my parents and my aunt Jan used another as a changing station. We arrived at the Duportail House early that day to get things set up. We were doing this on a shoestring budget, and that included making some of the food ourselves and setting up the event. As soon as we got to the Duportail House, we both asked if the air conditioning was on. It was, but it was an old system and it was fighting the 101-degree heat and to be accurate, the heat was kicking the shit out of the Duportail's air conditioning unit. Hence forth the Duportail House became known to us as the "Do or Die" house.

After a couple of hours, the Duportail House was transformed and ready for the wedding. There was a room for the ceremony (which then was cleared for dancing), a room for the bar, and a room to sit and eat. Val and I were soaked with sweat after setting things up. My parents, who had been helping, were also drenched. My parents left first for the hotel to shower and change. We were not far behind. We arrived, checked in, showered and changed. We even had enough time to relax before heading back. We decided to check in with my parents and my Aunt Jan to see if they were almost ready. My mother told me that they just arrived at the hotel. It had been almost 90 minutes since we left the Duportail House! It was two miles away. "How did it take you this long to go two miles down the road?" I asked. She said my father got lost and ended up on the Pennsylvania Turnpike going the wrong way. I sighed.

"Well," I said, "they are not starting without us. So, get changed and head over when you are ready." What else could I say? I told Val what happened. She looked at me incredulously then she remembered my father's incredibly unique ability to get lost at the drop of a hat. If there is anyone who can make a two-mile drive last 90 minutes and still believe that this was a natural thing, it was Sid.

Eventually it was time for the ceremony to begin. Our plan was to walk down the aisle together. To accomplish that feat, we had to wait upstairs while everyone got seated and we then wait for the music to begin. This is where the "Do or Die" truly lived up to its name, for while it was hot down on the main floor, it was a steam room upstairs. It was stifling hot. Perspiration dripped down our faces. With as much savoir faire as I could muster given the conditions, I turned to Val and said, "Are you ready to go live happily ever after?" Obviously, she said yes and we came downstairs. Well, we made it down the aisle without melting away to nothing, we read our vows, and were pronounced man and wife.

Twenty-six years later and still happy. That is not to say we haven't had a fight here or there, but we are happy together. Not a bad ending to the story.

Two quick side notes:

1. I explicitly told the DJ not to play the song "Celebration" by Kool & the Gang. I freaking hate that song. Well damned if someone didn't request it, and the DJ said that if they played it they would be fired. It may not be right to judge someone by their religion or by their political affiliation but if you like that song, you are dead to me.
2. Recall, if you will, that it reached 101 degrees on the wedding day and stayed hot well into the evening. Having said that, my parents loved hot coffee. They always wanted hot coffee, regardless of the temperature. The day of the wedding they were almost apoplectic that they couldn't get a working plug for the coffee pot. I had to laugh as I saw them running around trying to get the coffee going, while everyone was sweating generously. The only way to feel cool, was to go outside and feel how hot and muggy it was and then walk back inside. Does that sound like the time for a good steaming cup of Joe? Sigh!

Stay with Me because This is Brilliant

As I mentioned when discussing the title of this book, I have some very odd dreams. I will get back to that in a second but for now this:

Years ago, I read a book by Frederic Brown called "What Mad Universe." The book introduced me to the concept of the "multi-verse." The book was published in 1949 and presented the concept that there is not only more than one universe but there are an infinite number of universes. So, there is a universe where I do not exist (how boring that must be). There is one where I am writing this same book, this same passage in fact, but I am wearing purple socks (something unlikely for me in this universe). There is even a universe where you found the preceding two sentences funny. You get the gist. The concept has now gotten some traction in the scientific community and is considered a hypothesis worthy of study.

Now let's return to the subject of dreams. I have some very vivid dreams. I've battled demons and vampires. I have flown in planes that suddenly turned into roller coasters. I have flown without a plane. I have dreams so weird they defy adequate description. If Salvador Dali and M.C. Escher got together, dropped acid and then entered my brain, they might be able to provide a fair approximation of my dreams.

Most would say that these dreams are merely my subconscious wonderings, and while that could be true, what if as we sleep we are able to gently tap into the multi-verse and each dream we have is a veiled view into an alternate universe? It certainly explains my nocturnal mental wanderings but that would mean (as the old saying goes) the universe is not only stranger than we imagine, but it is stranger than we can imagine. I'm just saying. . .

The Honeymooners

We were off to St. Maarten for our honeymoon, at least that was the plan. The morning of the trip arrived, and we were all packed and ready to go. I called for a taxi the day before because our flight was early in the morning. As it turned out we were leaving on a weekday, and we knew we would have a little rush hour traffic to deal with, so we planned accordingly. What we didn't plan for was a taxi driver arriving 30 minutes late, unable to find his way down a straight street without getting lost, let alone find National Airport. Due to his general ineptitude, we were running late for our flight. We finally got out of the taxi (no tip for you buddy) and ran into the airport to check in.

We waited as patiently as we could in line, but we were nervous we would not make the flight. We finally got up to the counter and told the agent we were in a hurry and that we were trying to make our flight for our honeymoon. She gave us a look that clearly communicated that she didn't give a shit and proceeded to take her sweet old time checking us in. I remember pleading with her to please hurry. She continued to do her best imitation of a two-toed sloth as she got our bags and tickets processed. Finally, she finished and we ran to the gate. This was long before the days of enhanced security at our airports, so we could get to the gate pretty quickly. But we were too late. The plane had just pulled away from the gate and we were not going to St. Maarten that morning. Our luggage, however, was well on its way to the island. The woman at the gate was so slow getting us our tickets, but she had managed to get our bags checked through and on to the plane. I remember thinking that I hoped our bags would have a nice time at the resort without us.

I was now officially pissed. In fact, I was livid. No, strike that. I was well past livid, I was boiling. Imagine a volcano on Venus and multiply it a thousand-fold, and you would barely approximate the anger I was experiencing at that moment. First, I got Barney Fife for a taxi driver and then Nurse Ratched behind the airline counter – damn I was pissed. We walked back to the counter, Val was almost in tears. I walked straight up to Nurse Ratched who was busy being an ass to some other customer and barked at her, "Thanks to you we missed our flight. This, as I told you, is our honeymoon and you single-handedly may have just ruined it for us."

She frowned. "Sir," she said in a most dismissive tone, "May I give you my side?"

I cut her off before she could say another word, yelling "Lady, you don't get to have a side." Then Val and I walked away from her, with the hope of never seeing her again should we live to be a thousand years old.

We got back to the house and started re-arranging things. We called the airlines and gave them the story. They booked us on a flight for the very next day and gave us two free drink coupons, which didn't exactly make up for Nurse Ratched but it was something. Next, we called the hotel and they were kind enough to change our reservations so they began the next day in addition to holding our luggage for us. Next, I called the taxi company and gave them a piece of my mind. They provided us a Lincoln town-car and a knowledgeable driver for the next day at no expense.

We sat on the couch and convinced ourselves that this was not a bad omen and that the honeymoon (when we eventually got to the island) would still be great. As it turns out, it was a great honeymoon. Despite the inauspicious start, we had a great time.

One quick honeymoon anecdote about gambling on St. Maarten. I like to gamble a little, but Val was (at the time) not very familiar with gambling. On the honeymoon, I hit a hot streak. I literally could not lose. We went to the casino, and I won $800 in about an hour or so. I was so hot, just for shits and grins, I put $5 down on a single number on the roulette wheel and won on the first spin. One day, we headed to lunch and I paused before we went to the restaurant and played one game of blackjack and won. I turned to Val and said, "Lunch is on them."

As I said, Val was not too familiar with gambling, so near the end of the trip she turned to me and said, "Why don't you do this all the time? You might not need to work." I told her that this was a crazy fluke and this did not happen all the time. To prove that fact, several months later we were in Atlantic City and I lost $100 in five minutes at the blackjack table. Never tempt the Gambling Gods; they will smite you at the first opportunity!

Guilty as Charged

Let's talk about guilt. I am not talking about guilt in the criminal sense, but rather in more personal terms. I like to categorize guilt into two camps – Jewish Guilt and Catholic Guilt. Now mind you, you do not have to be Jewish or Catholic to have such guilt but I think Jews and Catholics exemplify these two different types of guilt the best.

Jewish Guilt is for shit you didn't do but should have. For example, your mother calls you on the phone and says, "I called you, so I assume you have a phone. I mean you must because we are talking now, so I am just wondering why you can't pick up the phone and call your mother once in a while? Would that be so painful? You should pick up the phone and make a call. It wouldn't kill you"

Here's another example, you're visiting a favorite aunt or a grandmother. You arrive and they look at you and say, "It's cold outside. You should have worn a heavier coat. You'll catch your death of cold out there!"

Catholic Guilt, on the other hand, is for shit you did do but shouldn't have. You go to confession for all the sins you racked up during the week and confess to all those darned impure thoughts you had! Combine the two and they got you both coming and going!

A Side of Bacon

Everyone has heard of the game Six Degrees of Kevin Bacon, where you try to tie an actor to Kevin Bacon in as few moves as possible. Well, I decided to take that just one step further and see if I could connect myself (however loosely) to Kevin Bacon.

As I have mentioned, I've met a great many political figures to include some past presidents but none of those meetings seemed likely to get me to Kevin Bacon. Then, I tried my meeting with Harlan Ellison as my starting point and bingo – Kevin Bacon! Let me show you the trail.

Harlan Ellison did a guest appearance (as himself) on an episode of The Simpsons back in 2014. One of the regulars on The Simpsons is an actor by the name of Hank Azaria. Mr. Azaria does dozens of voices on the show. Azaria has many other TV and film credits to include the movie "The Birdcage" back in 1996. That movie also starred a young Calista Flockhart. Now Flockhart also starred in a little-known movie called "Telling Lies in America" (1997) with none other than Kevin Bacon! Done in just four moves. I am so well-connected ☺

Superpowers

I have some random thoughts about superpowers that I feel compelled to share. Let's begin with a running debate in the Center Household between Val and I – not that we really care about the answer, but it is fun to joke about. The question on the table is this: While Batman is a superhero, does he truly have superpowers? I say that he most definitely does not, but Val contends that he does have some limited powers. Hit me on Facebook with your thoughts.

Several years ago, Val and I were in New York. We had spent the day taking my son to see the Spider-Man musical and were chilling out at the hotel bar. After a few drinks, the subject of superpowers naturally came up. I asked Val if she could choose a superpower what it would be, with the caveat that the superpower could not be one that is already taken by a known superhero. She pondered it, letting the question flow over her. She was really giving it some thought. Eventually, she said she wanted the power to instantaneously travel from one destination to another. Val hates traffic and traveling, so that made sense. While some superhero may have a similar power, I liked the response.

Now it was my turn. Now, let me preface, that my response, was infused with a great deal of alcohol, but I stand by it nevertheless. I said that I never wanted to have to go to the bathroom ever again – ever! Val looked at me with an expression equal parts amusement and befuddlement. I told her to think about it for a minute. Think about how much wasted time there is in a lifetime going to the bathroom, not to mention the inconvenience of having to go while on a plane, or while attending an important meeting, or while stuck in traffic. Think about it. No, this power will never help me defeat an evil villain or save the world, but I will leave those jobs to the comic book superheroes. As for me, I will be the guy sitting at the bar drinking a ton of beer and never having to leave my seat.

Your assignment is to go out to a local bar, have a few drinks, and then ask your friends the question. Results will vary depending on the amount of alcohol that is consumed before the question comes up.

Afterthought: While I haven't met anyone who can fly or leap tall building in a single bound, I have found that many of the people I know have some odd little superpowers. For example, my friend Rich can fall asleep in seconds. My friend Jeff has the incredible ability to consume vast amounts of alcohol and still function – he has a super liver! My friend Jim can seemingly quote lines from just about every popular movie ever made. My wife is a genuine empath. As for me, my superpower has got to be the silliest power in the world. I am tremendous playing those claw machines you see in arcades and in the front of family restaurants. Some are tough, but I am a master. So, if anyone needs a useless gizmo or a small stuffed animal, I am your man.

Fore!

In an earlier story, I mentioned that I've never gotten a hole-in-one. I am not a bad golfer (basically a bogey golfer), but having said that, itemized for your reading pleasure are some of my less than stellar moments on the golf course.

Greendale Golf Course: The 10th hole at Greendale is a sharp dogleg left. Down the right side of the fairway is the cart path, and about 200 yards out is a trashcan on the cart path. Most people aim straight ahead and try to land their drive about 225 yards out, at which point you can take your next shot at the green. One day, I teed up and hit a sky-high drive with a slight fade down the right-hand side of the fairway. It landed right into the trashcan by the cart path. I am not an expert on the rules of golf but I assumed that this counted as an unplayable lie! So, while I still don't have an official hole-in-one, I do have a trashcan-in-one. That was a pretty amazing shot.

Pinecrest Golf Course: Pinecrest is sort of an executive course with no hole longer than about 350 yards or so. The 4th hole is the longest hole, and you can take out a 3-wood off the tee. Running across the fairway are several telephone wires. I drove the ball high and straight and hit the top wire. My ball dropped straight down, on the fairway but only 150 yards out. Again, not a hole-in-one, but I have keen talent for finding the oddest obstacles.

Rock Creek Golf Course: I was golfing with my good friend Jim Ladd. We were playing on Rock Creek Golf course which is kind of hidden right in the District of Columbia. The day was hot, and we decided to take a golf cart. I hit a drive off the tee, and it went right into the woods. We were not sure if it was "findable," so I hit a provisional ball. After a minute or so of searching, we found my drive. So, we drove back out to the fairway to get my second drive (the second drive always finds the fairway, that is how the Golfing Gods operate). We approached the ball, and I was leaning out the cart to scoop it up as we slowed and drove by. Jim, believing I had already scooped up the ball made a hard-left turn to avoid a big dip in the fairway.

Unfortunately, I had not yet retrieved the ball and was, in fact, still leaning out the cart. He turned left, and I flew out of the cart onto the fairway. A true "America's Funniest Home Video," if someone had only caught it on their iPhone. Fortunately for me, neither existed just yet.

Penderbrook Golf Course: My friend Jim and I were on the 5th hole at this course. It is a medium range par three, around 180 yards or so. About 20 yards from the tee and off to the left is a ball washer. Well, I guess you can see where this story is going. I pulled the drive dead left and slammed the ball washer with a mighty blow. Jim ducked, cringed, and laughed all at the same time. I was dumbfounded and embarrassed but you know, stuff happens. The ball ricocheted onto the fairway and I put the next shot on the green – resulting some small measure of redemption.

Springfield Country Club: The 2nd hole on this course is a par five with a slight dogleg left. One morning, I hit a good drive and had about 200 yards into the green. I pulled out a 5-iron and took aim at the green. I pulled the shot into the greenside bunker on the left. As I walked up to the hole, I found a fox sitting calmly in the sand trap. He looked up at me and said in a very sarcastic voice, "Next time yell 'fore', and watch your *swing plane!*"

Hole #2 at Springfield with a very annoyed little fox.

Theme and Variation

In classical music, there is a form referred to as "Theme and Variation." In this form, the musical structure is built around a musical idea called the theme which is usually played at the start of the piece. The theme doesn't have to be especially long, but it is a recognizable musical melody. Once the theme is played, the composer begins to play with it by repeating it, but varying the theme in some fashion. This process gets repeated as many times as the composer chooses, producing a musical structure called 'Theme and Variation." Each variation (rhythm, tonality, harmony, instrument, etc.) is different, but can still be traced back to the original theme in some way.

It occurs to me that this is a rather apt allegory for life. We go through our days on a path. This is our chosen theme. Each of our days has a certain rhythm and tone to it. For example, I work in an office, I have meetings, I do a ton of reading, analysis, and writing in my work. I have a family, friends, hobbies and they too take on a certain predictable and enjoyable pattern. If the pattern was repeated ad nausea, I would be living in Bill Murry's "Groundhog Day" but life has its slight twists and turns which give us the variations to our theme. Not so much that the melody is unrecognizable but enough to make our lives interesting. For instance, I love the written word but taking on this little book was a wrinkle I had not anticipated several years ago. While this undertaking is not wholly inconsistent with my overall theme, it is a variation on that theme. It is the rare (and incredibly interesting) person indeed, who creates a whole different symphony in the midst of their life, and to them we have to tip our collective hat.

Trip to Israel and Egypt

In May of 1992, we took the trip of a lifetime to Israel and Egypt. We spent a week in Israel and then off to Egypt. I have some stories to share from that trip but before I do, I wanted to take just a moment to talk about history. As anyone who has traveled outside the U.S. can attest to, we Americans have a somewhat skewed perspective on history in the U.S. As a relatively young country, we tend to think of anything older than 200 years as truly historical. In truth, our history is but a mere flicker in the bonfire of history. Israel and Egypt offer a grander scale of recorded history and put our meager few hundred years into proper perspective.

El Al and the Never-Ending Journey into the Past

Val and I were going to Israel first, so we figured the logical choice was to fly El Al. It made sense that if you're flying to Israel, take the Israeli airline. Let's just say, this decision was on par with Brutus' decision to take credit for killing Julius Caesar. In my humble opinion, El Al was not a great airline. To be fair, they may be better now but back in 1992, they left something to be desired. The flight attendants didn't seem to get the concept of "customer service" and the seats on an EL Al airline were like sitting on cardboard and you were crammed into seats better suited for Tyrion Lannister.

It is a long flight from the east coast of the U.S. to Israel, about 10 hours minimum. We were so cramped and uncomfortable that I approached some folks sitting in the bulkhead seats to see if they would take $50 each for their seats. They looked back at our plight (crammed in like sardines) and shook their heads. I didn't blame them. About mid-way through the flight at about 30,000 feet, Val turned to me and said she had to get off the plane. I looked at her incredulously. "Val, I said, "I get it. You're uncomfortable, but we are 30,000 feet above the ocean. They can't just stop the plane and let us off."

She nodded. She knew it was a silly statement but she was that uncomfortable. She persevered through the rest of the flight and asked me to promise that we never fly El Al again. I said, "You bet." I knew we had booked round-trip tickets but figured I had two weeks to figure something out or purchase a horse tranquilizer for Val before she got on the plane to go home.

Jerusalem

We spent several days in and around Jerusalem and the Old City. Every sight and every sound spoke of a history tinged with turmoil and hope. Each sight from the Western Wall, to the Dome of the Rock, to the Church of the Holy Sepulcher was spectacular in their own way. We walked around the city on a wall that encircles the entire city. We came down off the wall in the Armenian Quarter right into the market area where we saw some sights you don't normally see on the tourist brochures. We saw animal carcasses being handled unceremoniously. We saw men busily engaging in all manner of trades and transactions. We did not blend in. I grabbed Val's hand and got us quickly back to more "tourist-like" surroundings as quickly as possible. We spent several days touring the Old City, and there was always more to see. One of the incongruities in the Old City are these little stores and shops that sit right next to many of the holy sites in the city. I recall seeing a little store right near the Western Wall, called "Off the Wall." The shop sold tacky little trinkets. It was, in my mind, somewhat inappropriate but it is not my city.

We stayed one night at a hotel in Jerusalem and a couple of nights at a kibbutz outside the city in the Judean Hills. Not far from the kibbutz was a restaurant that caught our attention. The name of the restaurant was "The Elvis Restaurant." We had to check it out. We walked in and saw, to our amazement, a restaurant that was a shrine to Elvis Presley. The walls were covered with pictures of Elvis – young Elvis, old Elvis, fat Elvis, rhinestone Elvis – they had them all. The camel out back was named Elvis! I would have expected something like this near Graceland (without the camel) but not in the hills of Judea. The proprietors spoke little English, so we never got a straight answer as to why they worshiped Elvis nor how the restaurant came to be. Just another mystery in a land full of them, I guess.

Learning to Shop

If you are in Israel's Old City or anywhere in Egypt, you need to learn a couple of important things about shopping. First, never point at anything you like. If you point at something, the shopkeeper will be all over you in seconds, and he will know you are interested. You had to feign disinterest at all times because every sale was a negotiation. If you didn't get the shopkeeper down at least 40 to 50 percent, you've been had. We learned the art of walking out of a shop, while falsely claiming no interest in some item we really wanted to buy. We would tell the shopkeeper that the item was not very good and that only a fool would buy such junk. We would tell him that we would be doing them a favor by taking it out of his shop. It was a game, an inside joke that both wise consumer and shop owner played with gusto. I loved the game once I understood the unwritten rules.

Land of the Pharaohs

Egypt was spectacular in every way. One night we went to the Sound and Light Show at the pyramids. They do the show just about every night, but each night the show is presented in a different language. We obviously selected the night it was done in English. I recall siting there with Val on that very special night. The temperature had cooled in the evening, and there was a nice little breeze; the evening was perfect. They began the light show, lighting up the pyramids with a deep voiced announcer providing the voice-over tale of the Pyramids of Giza. It all felt surreal. Here we were seated in front of the Pyramids of Giza, drinking a beer, and listening to the story unfold. Val and I knew it was a once in a lifetime moment and cherished it fully.

Driving in Cairo

Egypt is well known as the land of antiquities, but it should also be known as the craziest place to drive in the universe. Driving, and for that matter walking, in Cairo is not for the faint of heart. To get across the street you need to be a stunt actor, and to get across town you need to be a NASCAR Sprint Cup Champion (and yes, I had to look that up). There might be three traffic lights in all downtown Cairo. There were striped

149

lane markings on the streets that would indicate three or four cars across but these appeared to be mere suggestions, as we would often see seven or eight cars across. They jostled and bumped each other, and there seemed to be a whole language that existed with car horns – a Morse Code that I could not exactly decipher.

The Valley of the Kings and Queens, Luxor and Karnak

The two most awe-inspiring sites were Luxor and Karnak. These are two cites that time seems to have forgotten. The temples at Luxor and Karnak seem to jump out at you as you cross the desert. Huge edifices just seem to grow straight out of the ground. I do them a poor disservice by trying to capture the grandeur with mere words and even a picture does this place an injustice. Go and see them if you can.

At the Valley of the Kings we learned about Queen Hatshepsut from our guide. The queen was buried in the Valley of the Kings because she proclaimed herself Pharaoh. We nicknamed the queen "Queen Hot Chicken Soup" because if you spoke her name fast, it kind of sounded like that. We also saw the tombs of King Rameses the III and IV. It is amazing what has been preserved even after 3,000 years.

Coming Home

The time to leave both Egypt and Israel finally arrived. We had experienced so much that it was hard to leave. Harder still would be getting Val onto an El Al plane for the ride home. I never did get the horse tranquillizers, so I needed another option. I decided to upgrade us to Business Class. At the time, it was another $1,600 I didn't have, couldn't afford, and hated to part with but I told Val that ten years from now we would not miss the money. Both of us just didn't want to deal with the same flight from hell we had coming over. It was a smart move on our part. It turns out the El Al flight attendants are extremely nice when you fly Business Class. Also, the seats were comfortable; we could sleep or watch a movie at our leisure. It was definitely a good move.

Faith

Most of us say we have faith in God or some higher power. But, how many of us have a faith so strong that it is unbreakable? How many can say that their faith is so powerful that it guides their thoughts and actions, that it sustains them in times of despair, that it lifts them up, and even quells the fear of death?

I have met thousands of people and in all those interactions and relationships, I can only point to two people who I believe have a faith that strong. My friend Warner and my cousin Jackie are the only two people I know whose faith in God is so strong, so all encompassing, that it rises above belief and into the realm of fact. For them, God is as tangible as the chair you are sitting on right now. Theirs is not a "said" faith but a real faith.

Another facet that seems to differentiate people like Warner and Jackie, is that they do not see the need to proselytize their faith. I have had dozens of conversations with Warner about religion and God and all related matters. Warner is a Christian but he does not try to convert me. We talk as any two people would about what we believe and why. He and Jackie live their lives with a generous spirit and integrity, and hope that through this example, others might seek to live their lives in the same manner.

While I do not share their exact beliefs, I respect and admire them greatly.

Fatherhood

I grew up with a great father. I also grew up watching TV dads make fatherhood seem easy, so I figured being a dad would be a no brainer for guy as smart and wise as I believed myself to be. Not even close folks. I have two nice kids, don't get me wrong but being a parent is far from easy.

Watching Fred MacMurray ("My Three Sons") and Bill Bixby ("The Courtship of Eddie's Father") gave me the impression that all I had to do was calmly sit my kids down and have one of those famous heart-to-heart chats with my kids. We would hunker down, as Stephen King likes to say, and I would impart my kindly wisdom to inquisitive children. They'd listen and see the error of their ways, and everything would be fine. In the real world, where life stretches on for longer than 30-minute increments, problems just don't get resolved like that. I have had those talks with my boys and they listen; but, change happens inexorably slowly, and I would get frustrated at the pace. I remember writing to a friend the following one day when I thought it was all totally fruitless:

I am continually ignored. I am a mere electron spinning helplessly out of control. No, I am less than an electron for at least the tiny electron has a purpose and his role is clear. No for me, I am less than an electron. I am the imperceptible speck that hides in the quark that sits on the electron that swirls fruitlessly in search of nothing. To paraphrase the shortest verse in the Bible – and Brad wept.

I have two sons – Jeremy and Peter. As I write this, Jeremy is now 25 and Peter is 21. Hence, some of my work is now behind me, but you never stop being a parent. Jeremy is honest and hard working. He is also generally a reserved young man. Once you get to know him, he is funny and engaging, but he is generally a little on the shy side until then. Peter is a free spirit. He moves to his own beat and has an inner child that will probably never leave him. They are two good kids. I never had to worry about gangs, drugs, or any of that stuff. The only addiction is the computer and video game console. I guess I will take that.

Here are some vignettes involving my boys and life in "Parent Land." It is always interesting here in Parent Land. The roads can be a little rough and communication lines are not always reliable but generally the nation of Parent Land is not a bad place to live.

I Need a Beer

The kids were rather young, and we wanted to take a short trip during the summer. I believe Jeremy was around six and Peter around three. We ended up taking a short trip to Busch Gardens, which is a rather large amusement park about 100 miles south of us. We got there but the weather was not cooperating; it rained most of the day. What to do? We headed over to the Anheuser Busch brewery. Now before you start handing out the Worst Parents of the Year award to us, let me explain. We had heard that they give tours of the brewery and figured the kids might enjoy seeing the brewery/factory in action. It was something to do! We got there and the tour began soon enough, but they forgot to tell us that most of the brewery was not in operation that day. There was just not a ton to see. Jeremy was fairly interested because he always liked machines and seeing how they work. Peter not so much. About halfway through, Peter started getting cranky, and it got worse and worse. Nothing seemed to console him and eventually it erupted into a full-blown meltdown of epic proportions. To say that he started to cry would be a vast understatement. He was in a stroller, but he was thrashing about like a shark caught in net. This was not good. We rolled that stroller as quickly as we could to the exit at the end of the tour, but it took some time to get there. At the end of the tour, they offered a free sample. Val and I took one as soon as it was offered and got the hell out of there.

Peter, unfortunately, kept right on screaming and generally making life miserable. I recall quietly thinking, "If only we could have given Peter a beer." I let the thought go – not good parenting protocol. "Parent Land" basically sucked that morning. We had no idea what was making him miserable, but we were starved and so we stopped to get something to eat, hoping that maybe some food would make us and Peter a little happier. We were prepared to get the heck out of the restaurant real quick if Peter didn't settle down. Peter got one gulp of food in his mouth and was as happy as could be. Apparently, that is all he wanted, some hot food. We had tried to give him a snack at the brewery but he wasn't ready at that point to eat anything because he was so upset.

From that day forward we always compared any meltdown the kids had to the Anheuser Busch incident. None has ever lived up to that one.

A Pox on Our House

When Jeremy was around five or so he got the chicken pox. It was a very bad case. I remember putting mittens on his hands to prevent him from scratching. We did the infamous oatmeal baths. We put medications on him, in him, around him – nothing helped that much. Val is generally better in the mornings and I am better at night, so we traded shifts trying to keep him happy and occupied. One night I was up with him, and it was a bad night. He was miserable. The only thing that seemed to keep him happy was watching the movie "The Land Before Time." I think we watched that movie five times that night but it made him less unhappy. I was bat shit crazy after five showing of "The Land Before Time" but it did the trick for him. While I have no desire to ever see that film again, it has a soft spot in my heart because it kept Jeremy happy that night.

Helter Skelter

When Peter was around seven, he had his tonsils taken out. The surgery went well and he was in his bed that night. The next two days passed without incident, but on the third night Peter walked into our bedroom late at night and said he had just thrown up. Val asked him if he was OK and he said he was fine and proceeded to lie down on the floor of our bedroom and fall right back to sleep. Val got up to check the damage. She wasn't sure if Peter had gotten to the bathroom or not so she walked down the hall to check both the bathroom and his bedroom. She came flying back to our bedroom in a panic.

She said, "Brad, you had better come see this." I groggily got out of bed and came to see what all the fuss was about. I went into Peter's bedroom.

There was blood everywhere. I would have thought the Manson family had visited our house. We went into the bathroom – same thing. I check on Jeremy. I had to make sure all this blood had come from Peter. It seemed inconceivable. Jeremy was fine. We went back to check on Peter. He was sleeping calmly on the floor. Val checked his breath and pulse, and both were normal. Val called the doctor's office and left a message with his service. We were about to go to the emergency room when he called us back and told Val to take him to the hospital and that he would meet her there. The doctor said that despite the horrific scene Peter probably had some blood that had been dripping from the incision down into his stomach and it had built up over a couple of days and he just threw it up. He wanted to examine him to make sure the bleeding had stopped, but most likely he would be OK.

Val went off with Peter to the hospital and I stayed behind to begin (somehow) to try to clean this mess up. I wasn't even sure where or how to begin. There was blood on the carpets, in the bed, on just about every surface I looked at. I considered just putting the house up for sale that night rather than attempt to clean this. Of course, I don't think the resale would be that strong with all the blood. No perspective buyer would believe this was simply a case of a tonsillectomy gone bad. It took hours to make any progress.

Val came back several hours later, and Peter was fine. His bedroom and bathroom were another matter. We had to get new carpet, new bedding, and a new bath mat. There was no saving this stuff with all that blood. To this day, I have no idea how such a small child with such a minor post-op issue could produce so much blood.

A Child's "plee-sting"

What? "A child's plee-sting" was a phrase Jeremy kept saying for a full week. We had no idea what he was talking about but it was his favorite line. He would point to something and say the phrase. One day, Jeremy asked Val to put "Toy Story" on the TV and watch with him. Val popped the tape into the VCR and the movie started to play. About halfway through the movie, Woody turns to Buzz and tells him he is nothing but a "child's plaything." Val jumped up, spun, and turned to Jeremy. "Is that what you have been saying?" He nodded, thinking *of course that is what I have been saying. Haven't you been paying attention?* Mystery solved.

The Jungle Book

I think it is safe to say that Disney's "The Jungle Book" is a classic. Peter fell in love with the movie from the start. There are some very funny and entertaining characters in the story to include Bagheera (the serious black panther), Baloo (the good-time singing bear), and King Louie (the fire seeking orangutan), but Peter did not connect deeply with any of these characters. However, there is a scene in the movie where a small herd of elephants march through the jungle and happen upon Mowgli. Peter loved the elephants. For years, he was fascinated by all things elephant. When we would go to the beach, Val would draw an elephant in the sand with a stick and he would be spellbound and delighted. He watched "The Jungle Book" over and over, and any nature show that featured elephants was an instant favorite. Then, several years later we noticed the fascination was gone. It had just evaporated like the dew in the summer sun. We could not catalogue it on a specific date or event, but one day we asked him if he still liked elephants and he said not especially. He didn't have anything against them but the attachment was gone. It seems that kids have the capacity to shift and adapt more frequently and easily than adults. Their journey contains various detours and tangents that form the pathways of their brain. I guess elephants were an enjoyable tangent for Peter.

Open Your Mouth and Say "Ahhh"

When Jeremy was around two or three, he was playing quietly in the living room, and I needed to go upstairs for a minute or two. I leaned down to him and told him that I was going upstairs and would be right back. He nodded. I was gone for no more than a minute or so. I came down and looked at Jeremy and knew immediately that something wasn't quite right. He didn't say a word, he just starred up at me with a look that told me something was amiss. On instinct, I said open your mouth. He complied. In that instant, my son had turned into a human slot machine. Quarters poured from his tiny mouth. Apparently, while I was upstairs, he had found some quarters that Val or I had been putting into rolls for the bank. He probably had stuffed a dozen quarters in his mouth while I was gone. Fortunately, I hit the jackpot and all the quarters were returned and none swallowed.

About seven years later, we were not so lucky. Peter was about five and he was upstairs in our bed watching TV. Val and I were downstairs attending to some odds and ends before coming upstairs to put Peter to bed. As we came in, Peter looked over to us and said he had just swallowed the "light thingy." We had no idea what a "light thingy" was, but it wasn't on his diet plan, I can tell you that much. He looked fine and acted OK, so we didn't panic but we were still concerned. What the heck had he swallowed? He wasn't choking and seemed fine, but it was disturbing. I went to turn out my lamp that sits on the bedside end table and noticed the knob from the lamp on the table was gone. He had swallowed the knob!

We didn't panic, although panicking would not necessarily have been a bad option, but we took him to the doctor and they examined him. The x-ray clearly showed the knob. The good news was that the round part of the knob was pointed downward, and the doctor said it should (how should I say it?) come out naturally in the next 24 hours. Well that's what happened – no harm/no foul. I will spare you the less than joyful aspects of checking to see that the knob had passed through my child's system. But as the old saying goes – this too shall pass!

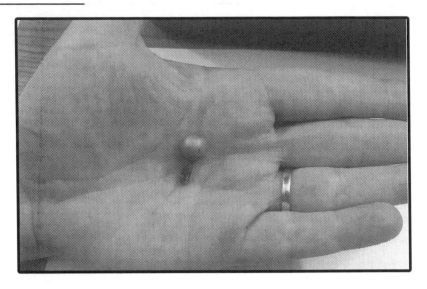

The offending light switch – picture taken well after this incident.

Running for Gold

Peter is not the major athlete. It's just not his bag. He is a big kid and strong but playing sports and aerobic exercise are as likely a pairing as Donald Trump and Hillary Clinton on the dance floor together. That doesn't stop Val from trying to get Peter to exercise and get in some physical activity. For a couple of years, she was able to get Peter to compete in our local Special Olympics. Especially surprising was her ability to get Peter to compete in an 800-meter dash. Now in the Special Olympics, it is not quite a dash but no need to dwell on that part. Peter started out and was keeping pace for about half the event. As they started on the second half, the race turned into a two-way competition between Peter and a young girl. Because Peter rarely competes in athletic events, he is not used to success in such endeavors. Suddenly, you could see in his eyes that he could actually win this race. Val and I were in the stands and started cheering as loudly as we could in the hopes that it might push him. He started closing the gap between him and the young girl. Peter put on a last push and won the race. He was exhausted and elated in equal measure. But more than exhaustion and elation was a general sense of amazement. He had actually done it. He had come from behind and won an athletic competition. Of course, those emotions wore off quickly, and then he wanted off that hot track and into someplace with gosh darn air conditioning!

Snowpocalypse

Jeremy drives a truck providing support to construction crews in our area. However, in the winter his company provides road service during winter storms. Jeremy plows, salts, and sands the roads. When the snow is bad, he can be out on the roads for days at a time. A couple of years ago we had a bad storm. The newscasters nicknamed it "Snowpocalypse," since a few years earlier they had named another storm "Snowmageddon." I imagine the next one is likely to be "Snowzilla."

Jeremy knew he would be out for a couple of days and since he was working about 20 miles from the house, he got a hotel room to use as his base of operations. He called us on day two of the storm and said that he needed a favor. He was trying to clear out his car from the hotel parking lot so he could get to the depot where his snow plow was waiting for him. He got halfway out, but no further. The car was stuck. He called his boss and they sent another driver to pick him up from the hotel but his car was in the middle of the hotel lot and needed to be moved.

Jeremy was now in a large convoy of trucks plowing the roads and couldn't just stop to resume digging out his car, so he called us for help. We were 20 miles away and it was snowing but we were his only option. We called the hotel, and the manager explained that they wanted to clear a path in the parking lot so others could get out. Val and I looked at each other and said, "Let's do our best. It's sure to be an adventure."

First, we got Peter and our neighbors to help dig out our driveway so we could get our car out. After 20 minutes or so we were out and moving. We brought a couple of shovels with us to dig out Jeremy's car. We got on I-95 going south, averaging about 25 miles per hour. The snow was coming down, and the roads were treacherous. However, the worst of it was the trucks flying down the highway, not seeming to care that we had a foot of snow on the ground. We eventually got to his hotel, and with the assistance of the hotel manager got Jeremy's car back into his spot so the plow could do its job on the parking lot. Then it was back on the highway and time to head for home. About three miles before we reached the house, the snow picked up speed and the winds started whipping hard. It was whiteout conditions! I was basically guessing where the road was, but there was no way I was stopping in these conditions. We pushed on, and made it; but it was pure luck. If we had crashed, we would probably look back at the day as a mess, but since we didn't we simply chalked it up as an adventure – one that worked out for everyone (Jeremy, his company, the hotel manager and guests, and us). Somedays, I guess God is smiling down at you.

Uncle-Hood

So, there is Jeremy, and there is Peter, but no little girl in the house. That was the case until about seven years ago when a friend of Valerie's had a little girl, Ana. Val and I are kind of Ana's surrogate aunt and uncle. She stays over at our place often, and even goes on vacation with us when we go "down to the shore." She's adorable, and she knows it. Every time you take her picture, she does a pose like she is a professional model. The great thing about being a surrogate aunt and uncle is that we don't have the everyday responsibilities of parenting. We don't spoil her, but she does get to do the fun stuff with Aunt Val and Uncle Brad. It's a good gig.

The family at Disney in 2016.

Ana and the gang at Ocean City New Jersey in 2017.

Philosophy 101

It may have been Socrates who once said, "the unexamined life is not worth living." Of course, Socrates didn't get out much and was an absolute bore at parties. But, having said that I generally agree with him. At some point, you begin to either formally adopt a set of philosophies that guide your thinking or they sort of creep up on you like ivy on an old home.

In the end, you must ask yourself, "What do I believe, and why?" The answers may evolve over time, or they may not, but I think it is a good practice to challenge your long-held beliefs from time-to-time and see if they still feel right to you.

I kind of categorize myself as a Deist, Taoist, Utilitarian, and Jew – mix all those altogether like some philosophical stew, and you kind of have what I believe. You can throw some elements of Christianity, Buddhism, and Zen into the stew – sort of the spice to the stew that adds just the right amount of flavor.

Without some type of anchor to help ground us, I think we tend to drift and lose our way. Our philosophy or world view can help keep us centered and help us understand the world around us – enabling us to put things in their proper context. Without that anchor, we begin to see ourselves as inconsequential, irrelevant, and immaterial.

I could go on for pages about my specific beliefs but let's face it, I am no Socrates, I can already see you starting to lose focus and attention on this little diatribe. Turn the page and you'll find an entertaining story, but before that, remember the words of Max Weber who once said:

"It is immensely moving when a mature man - no matter whether old or young in years - is aware of a responsibility with heart and soul. He then acts by following an ethic of responsibility and somewhere reaches the point where he says: 'Here I stand; I can do no other'. That is something genuinely human and moving. And every one of us who is not spiritually dead must realize the possibility of finding himself at some time in that position."

Hershey Park Hell

I grew up with two amusement parks that we loved to visit when we got the chance, which given our family finances, wasn't too often. One was Dorney Park and the other was Hersheypark. Hersheypark was the bigger attraction and the one we coveted the most. I have very fond memories of both parks.

My wife's sister lives in Hanover, Pennsylvania, which is not far from Hershey, PA. We were planning a trip to visit her sister anyway, and so I got the brilliant idea to combine the visit with a short trip to Hershey. Our kids were with us for the trip, and they were the perfect age for Hersheypark.

It was a Saturday afternoon and we headed off for Hershey from Hanover. We were about 15 miles from Hershey when I stopped at a red light. I waited to turn right up a small hill onto U.S. # "Who Gives a Crap" and hit the gas as the light turned green. The van started to pull forward and suddenly stopped dead. We started coasting a little around the turn, but we weren't moving much at all. The engine was working, as I could hear it, but there was no movement forward because my transmission had decided it had no intention of going to Hersheypark. The car, apparently, was allergic to chocolate and had no intention of going any further.

I got Val into the driver's seat and my older son Jeremy and I pushed the van (a Chevrolet Venture) up the hill and into the nearest commercial driveway, which turned out to be a GM Dealership! I was in luck, I figured. I was wrong. The dealership apparently had closed for the day. So, we called for a tow truck and had the van towed to a nearby towing company. I remember asking the how much for the tow, and it was a reasonable price. I also asked him if we could leave the car while we go to Hershey and figure out our next move. He said, "no problem." Therefore, we left the towing company and caught a cab to the hotel.

This was a bit of a hiccup, but we figured we would make the best of it. The next day at Hershey, we spent the day on some rides with the kids and intermittently making calls to our insurance company and to arrange for a rental car.

The day at Hershey was alright, I guess, but somethings might be better left in the past. After going to Disney and Universal, Hershey just isn't quite the exciting place I remembered as a kid. I guess the title of this story is a bit misleading because Hershey itself wasn't the problem. The problems really started when we got home.

I called a local GM Dealer on Monday and asked about the cost for a transmission for the van. They told me it would cost around $2,500. I didn't want to put that much into the van because it was already five or six years old. So, Val and I went to a local Kia dealership and bought a new Kia Sedona (a.k.a. another boring minivan). The Kia dealership said they would take the crippled Chevy Venture as a trade-in, knowing it needed a new transmission. They didn't offer me much for the Chevy but given its condition, I took it. They told me that they needed a day or two to run up to Dillsburg, PA (where the towing company was located) to pick up the van. Val called the towing company and they said they would hold on to it for a few more days. No problem. This is where things turn out badly for the Center Clan.

Val called the insurance company to get the new Kia set up. In the process of the conversation, the woman from GEICO asked Val if she wanted to purchase an extended warranty on the Kia like we had on the Chevy Venture. Val said, "What extended warranty?" The woman from GEICO told Val that we purchased an extended warranty on the Chevy when we first insured it and that it would have covered most of the cost of the new transmission.

Val told the woman from GEICO, "Don't tell me that now after we just bought a new car! Why didn't anyone happen to mention that to us when we called about the reimbursement for the rental car?" Basically, we bought a new car when I could have gotten the Venture fixed for around $500 not $2,500. We colossally fucked that up. But the fun didn't stop there.

A couple of days later, the Kia dealership called to tell me that they were trying to pick up my car from the towing company but the company would not release the van until the bill was paid. I told them that I had paid for the tow of the van the day it broke down. I then got on the phone with the owner of the towing company, and he told me that I owed him an additional $500. I asked him why and he informed me that there was a $500 fee for storing the car there for the last five days. I was apoplectic. I told him that when the car broke down, I asked him if it would be any problem if I left the car there for a couple of days, and that my wife asked if we could leave it there until the Kia dealership picked it up and both times we were told it was not a problem. He laughed and said it was not a problem but there is a $500 charge! Funny guy. I told him that it might have been nice to mention that charge at some point during the conversations. He said that there was a sign behind his counter that indicates that there will be a charge for cars left on the lot. I didn't recall seeing a sign but he said it was there. If that sign existed, my guess is that you would need super-vision to make out what it said. It was probably thirty feet behind the counter and written in the tiny lettering you see at the bottom of the Eye Chart. In the end, I had to pay the bill but I told the guy he was absolute scum and asked him how he slept at night. He said, "As long as I have your money, I will sleep like a baby." What an asshole.

So, in the end, the trip to Hershey cost me a heck of a lot of money. Moral of the story:

- Know what insurance/warranty coverage you have on your car!
- Never leave your car at a towing company longer than you absolutely must.
- Never speak of Hersheypark again.

Poetic Pomposity

When I was much younger, I remember sitting down to write a series of holiday cards. For each card, I tried to write something from the heart – something that was meaningful. It was hard work. Then it occurred to me that I should come up with a saying or some type of holiday/New Year greeting that was my very own. Once completed, I could pop it into every card. I could be deep and insightful and efficient all in one fell swoop. I did just that, and I even sent out a few cards with the words below inscribed. Problem solved – or so I thought.

The next time I was in the situation, I pulled out the saying and here was the problem. What I thought was poetic, wise, and insightful now sounded pompous, hackneyed, and trite. It was like I had kept a piece of food in the refrigerator too long and when I took it out, it smelled bad. With great trepidation, I submit that little saying to you now. I thought I was being wise and spiritual at the time. Try not to judge me too hard. I was young.

Why reject the unknown – when you can explore it.
Why defend the status quo – when you can expand it.
Why attack problems – when you can engage them.
Why change for the sake of change – when you can evolve for some higher propose.

Why merely survive – when you can live.
After all the choice is yours

My Dear Departed Brother Dave. . .

As you walk into the Haunted Mansion at Walt Disney World, you pass a series of silly gravestones. One of these gravestones bares the inscription "My Dear Departed Brother Dave. He Chased a Bear into a Cave." I always smiled as I passed that one at Disney because of my brother. My brother and I would joke about it. I still smile, but now that smile helps me deal with the pain of my brother's passing.

It was no bear that got my brother – no, it was that evil bastard cancer that got him. Cancer is an insidious monster. It's a malevolent force, and it is pure fucking evil. It has taken my father, my brother, and many good friends over the years. I hate it.

Talking about my brother remains painful to this day, even seven years after his death. He was 50 years old when he died, and he was cheated out of the remainder of what was a good life with family and friends who cared deeply about him.

My brother was diagnosed with lung cancer. It metastasized to his brain about six months later. He died after a two-year fight with this sinister beast. During those two years, we spent time talking and dealing with an outcome we both knew was coming. I tried to lighten his load where I could, but there is only so much you can do.

Near the end, I got a call from his hospice team that he'd had a stroke and that the time was near. I immediately headed to his home outside Philadelphia. I walked into his bedroom and knew instantly that this was the end. The stroke had hit him hard. He couldn't talk and I am not 100 percent sure if he knew I was there or not. I spent the next several hours just sitting at his bedside talking to him. I told him that he could let go. I told him that I had everything handled, and Regina (his ex-wife) would be there for his two sons Ben and Noah. I told him that if Regina, Ben, or Noah ever needed anything that I would make sure they got it. I have no idea if he heard a single word I said or not. I hope he did. I can believe that, can't I? Perhaps he heard me after all because he died just 10 hour later.

There was no final deathbed scene like you see in the movies or on TV. I tend to doubt anyone ever gets that type of poetic goodbye. At the end, all we have is the memories of the person who once lay in the bed we now stand over, and pray that the end was without pain and fear.

An Intense Columnar Vortex

Val and I took a trip to the Bahamas a few years back. Part of the vacation included a snorkeling trip. We boarded a medium sized boat with about 20 or so other tourists and headed out to a very small island for some good snorkeling and a picnic lunch. The boat dropped us off at a beautiful beach and told us that they would dock over on the other side of the island. They told us that at the top of the island was an old fort where we would meet for lunch in 90 minutes.

Into the ocean we went. The snorkeling was fine, as best as I can recall. My memory on the snorkeling is somewhat fuzzy because of what happened next. Val and I must have been in the water only 15 minutes or so, when we both sensed something. It may have been a slight drop in temperature. It may have been a sudden breeze on our backs. Hell, it may have been our Spidey Senses, but whatever the cause we both picked our heads up from snorkeling at the same instant and looked out to sea. We froze.

About a mile off the island were two waterspouts. What a nice, fun little name that is for what was out there. For those unaccustomed with the term, a waterspout is an intense columnar vortex on the water, otherwise referred to by us land-lubbers as a *fucking tornado*. Val and I decided that getting out of the water would be a freaking marvelous idea at this juncture. We and the other members of the trip gathered on the beach for a minute when we remembered about the fort at the top of the island. We decided that it would offer some protection and seemed a shit load smarter idea than hanging out on the beach. It took us about ten minutes to climb up to the fort, all the while keeping an eye on those waterspouts.

We arrived at the fort and it looked as though it would provide some safety if things got rough. The top of the island also provided us with a panoramic view. We looked down to where our boat was supposed to be docked. It was gone! We turned back to look at the waterspouts. They were moving fast now, but the angle looked like it would carry them just past the western edge of the island. We crossed our fingers. We waited. They passed the island, missing us by a half a mile. We continued to watch them as they both slowly started to dissipate and lose their twister shape. At this point, there was no reason to go back down to the beach, so we waited for the crew to return with lunch. The boat came back in a few minutes and the crew made their way up to the fort. Some members of our snorkeling party were really pissed.

"Why the hell did you leave?" they yelled.

The captain replied, "I needed to get the boat out of the way of the storm, so we all had a way of getting off the island after the waterspouts had gone. We get them all the time. No worries."

That explanation actually made sense to me but there were some folks who were still angry and this explanation did not placate them. For Val and me, we just had to smile and chalk it up as another adventure – especially since the danger had passed.

Vanity – My Favorite Sin

Did you ever see the movie 'The Devil's Advocate?" Near the end of the film, Pacino reiterates a line that is central to the movie. He says, as only Pacino can, "Vanity, definitely my favorite sin."

While it may be a bit embarrassing to admit, I am a tad vain, at least in one specific area. I do not want to go bald. I realize I am fighting a battle I will eventually lose, but for now I still have close to a full head of hair, well almost. I do not need to try to pull off (nor would I ever) the oh so stupid comb-over fiasco like our current President. It is hard for me to imagine that he looks in the mirror and says to himself, "Gee that looks good." If there was ever a big fucking warning sign, way before the election, it should have been that. Can we really trust someone's judgement who honestly thinks that hairdo looks good? But I digress.

My father lost his hair by the time he was thirty. My brother lost his completely by the time he was forty. My own hair started to thin when I hit forty, but I was not going to go quietly into the good night. I got a hair transplant. It went well. These days, the procedure is much easier and hard to detect. I did the first transplant on a Thursday and was back to work on Monday and no one could tell. At that time, my hair hadn't thinned to the point where such a procedure would be obvious. It worked so well that about five years later I did it again. Big mistake – gargantuan in fact!

Unlike the first procedure where there was no pain, I noticed this time there was some pain in the back of head in the donor area. I called the doctor's office, and they said that this was nothing to worry about. The guy I spoke to was not the doctor. He was wrong. He was very fucking wrong.

About a week or two after the second procedure, things went terribly awry. I came home from a long day at work and felt like taking a shower. I was in the shower and Val was downstairs cooking dinner when my head started bleeding. Apparently, during the procedure the doctor had nicked an artery, and the pain I felt was the blood collecting behind my head and pushing against the skin. Now that spot burst open and blood started

171

pouring out. It was like the scene from "Pyscho," except this was in living color, and I had done this to myself.

I started pounding on the shower floor with my foot hoping to get Val's attention – no luck. Somehow, I managed to put enough pressure on my head to stem the bleeding for a moment so I that could wrap a towel around my head. I yelled for Val. She came upstairs, and I told her what was happening.

She asked, "Do you think we should call an ambulance?"

I thought about for a second and said, "Yes, I think we'd better." At that point, my head started bleeding again, and Val had to rewrap the towel and apply additional pressure to get the blood to stop. There was blood all over the bathroom and our bed.

Val then called the ambulance and they told us they would be there in about 10 minutes. Val turned to leave and make arrangements for the kids with our neighbors, but at the last minute I called out to her, "Help me get some underwear and pants on! I am not letting the ambulance personnel find me naked and bleeding if I can help it." See, vanity is most definitely my sin.

The ambulance arrived on time, and they came upstairs. Val explained the situation. There were two ambulance workers, and one was a woman so I was happy (relatively speaking) that I had asked Val to help me get my pants on. The lead ambulance worker (let's call him Fred) told Val that he wanted to have a quick look at the back of my head before they left for the hospital. Val warned him that it was a bad move because blood would spurt out like Mt. Vesuvius but Fred didn't listen. He jumped back after getting hit with blood in the face and said, "That's an arterial bleed — he needs to go to the hospital!" Val said, "Yeah, why do you think we called for an ambulance?" The female ambulance worker (let's call her Wilma) helped Fred wrap up my head until I resembled a wise old Sikh. Fred and Wilma got me on a stretcher and out to the ambulance. By that time, our neighbors (Debra and Dan) had come down to grab the kids. Off I went in the ambulance, and Val was not too far behind in her car.

I was rushed into the emergency room and an emergency room doctor got to me very fast. We'll call him Barney for obvious reasons. About the time he was about to unwrap my makeshift turban, Val arrived. Val told Barney what would happen if he unwrapped the towel and bandages. He looked at her as if she was a worried wife who was prone to exaggeration. He too jumped back with a bloody face. Val looked around like "is anyone ever going to believe me?" Then the real fun began.

Barney and his nurse (of course we will call her Betty) worked diligently to stem the bleeding, but it was slow going. Barney kept apologizing to me that he couldn't stop the bleeding. The nicked artery was hard to reach and was a slippery little devil. I told him not to worry and just get hold of the damn thing and stop the bleeding. I would feel extremely silly, I told him, dying from a botched hair transplant. Meanwhile Betty had to attend to another patient and Val ended up assisting the doctor by handing him absorbent bandages to soak up the blood. Val is a physical therapist and has some experience with blood, doctors, and hospitals, so she handled it like a pro. Finally, he managed to stop the bleeding and began stitching it up. Mind you, all of this occurred without any anesthesia. He got near the end and told me that he had to finish the job with a staple or two. *Great, perfect ending,* I thought. Val told me later that even she turned her head for the final stapling.

They bandaged me up and sent me home. I survived. That was in 2006. I am happy to report I still have some hair after all of that but probably not for too much longer. I kind of think another hair transplant is unlikely. I am vain, but I am not totally stupid.

I Was Wrong

Just to be clear, I don't often admit to being wrong. But back in 1996, I turned out to be wrong on a titanic scale. Val and I went to the movies and we saw a trailer for the movie "Titanic." I watched the trailer and told Val unequivocally that this movie would bomb. I told her it had "Heaven's Gate" written all over it. It looked like a big, gaudy, schmaltzy mess. Depending upon one's point of view, it may have been one or all of those, but a bomb at the box office, it most certainly was not.

After the movie broke all kinds of box office records, Val was compelled to remind me of this slight error in judgement. I, of course, never wanting to let a good opportunity to be obnoxious go to waste told her that I had not been wrong. I may have momentarily misspoken but I was clearly not wrong. I told her that the Dali Lama frequently called and asked me for spiritual advice and that Warren Buffet called for financial advice. I told her that I have secretly been writing the Dear Abby advice column for many years. I told her I had helped Thomas Paine write "Common Sense."

I said, "Does that sound like a person who was mistaken?"

Val said, "No it sounds like a person who is mentally unstable."

"Possibly," I said, "but not wrong."

Virginia's Wonders of the World

Val and I were trying to decide what do for summer vacation one year. For various reasons, we wanted to keep expenses on this trip to a minimum, so I told Val to see what she could find that was somewhat local. The kids were still young, so if we found the right spots locally they would be just fine.

That was all it took, and Val was off to the races. She started digging and after a week or two of research, planned the oddest little vacation for us that I can imagine. Our adventure included a nice visit to the Natural Bridge, which is a tranquil and beautiful place. Our next stop was Professor Cline's Haunted Monster Museum & Dark Maze. It was total kitsch and stupid but fun nevertheless. Next, we wanted (as any good tourist would) to visit Foamhenge. What exactly is Foamhenge? Why, it is an exact replica of Stonehenge made from foam. How could anyone pass up such a wondrous sight? Unfortunately for us, Foamhenge was undergoing some minor renovations and all we could do was see it from afar. My bucket list will obviously remain incomplete until I can experience the majesty of Foamhenge up close. I daresay this great unnatural wonder is on everyone's bucket list.

The next day we visited the Virginia Safari Park. I am not sure exactly what we were expecting – maybe a nice little petting zoo or maybe one of those places you drive through and see the animals from afar, safe inside your vehicle. However, the Virginia Safari Park was, well more like a safari. They allow you to drive through the park and actually feed the animals. While there were no lions or other inherently dangerous animals, they had zebras, camels, bison, watusi cattle, yaks, etc. Noah would have felt right at home, except there was no ark.

Not only do they allow you to drive right on through at your own pace, but you can also purchase food to give to the animals. Per the brochure, you just roll down the window and give them a little food. And, what the hell, they're right. We had driven no more than 100 feet when I rolled down the window, and very large bison stuck his head through. I was dumbstruck.

He started looking around for food and snorting. He also started drooling all over me. I cracked up.

I shouted over to Val, "He's drooling all over me. What the hell do I do?"

She's cracking up hard too, but managed to shout back, "Feed him, quick before he eats the steering wheel!"

We spent the next thirty minutes driving through the park. The llamas and zebras were better behaved but the watusi cattle and yaks, not so much. At some point an ibex stole a whole cup of food out of my son's hand. The animals had this gig down cold. They knew that when a window was down, food was coming! It was a hysterical. I would not advise anyone taking a really nice car or SUV into the park unless you don't mind drool in your car and assorted nibbling of your vehicle.

The following day we were off to a llama trek. Yes, that's right, there is a place Virginia where you can arrange to walk around some pastures with your own personal llamas. The owners were a nice older couple who figured this was an entertaining way to supplement their income. The old man, we will call him Old Man Fordham, gave us a quick introduction to llama-handling, to include a discussion about llama spitting. They apparently do that on occasion, although we were lucky in that respect (we had little spitting action during the day). After the orientation, Old Man Fordham introduced us to our llama partners for the day. Val was given a rambunctious fellow named Jonas. My llama was named Happy. Peter got Chaos and Jeremy got a llama named Jack. Off we went, the four of us, our llamas, Old Man Fordham, and his three dogs. About halfway through, the dogs started chasing a squirrel, which spooked Val's llama, Jonas. Old Man Fordham and I had to chase down Jonas who had bolted out of Val's grip. After we got him back in the fold, I gave Val my llama (Happy) to walk and I took the rambunctious Jonas. As we neared the end of the trek, Happy started to give Val some trouble, and off he went. Old Man Fordham got hold of him, and Val finished the walk sans llama. After we completed the walk, we took some pictures with the llamas. Happy started to hum around Val, which she took as an apology for being hard to handle near the end of the walk – and all was forgiven.

It was one of our favorite trips of all time thanks to Val. She managed to find some quirky and unique spots for the family to visit. We have traveled to some great vacation destinations over the years, but this goofy little trip around Virginia had more laughs than any other trip we've taken.

One of the watusi cattle trying to stick his head inside the car.

Here is Val with the llama Happy.

PART 9

Interlude Two – Excerpt from Refracted Image

In the Acknowledgments section of this book I thanked my friend Richard Kosoff who wrote a similar book several years ago and planted the seed for this effort. In that acknowledgement section I tend to give the impression that this is the only reason for this literary effort. But if the truth be told (which it seldom is), there is another reason. While writing this book has been a challenge, it is a shit load easier than trying to finish my half-written novel called *Refracted Image*. Part of me longs to get back to that novel and part of me fears going back to it. I have let it languish for several years and I am not sure how best to proceed. Additionally, writing a novel is an arduous task – significantly harder than this memoir. At least this is the case for me. Therefore, just in case I don't find my way back to the book relatively soon or ever, let me present within the confines of this memoir, just a portion of the book. This way at least part of it will see the light of day.

Let me quickly set the stage here because I am selecting two portions of the book that do not connect. The first selection is naturally the first few pages of the book and I will let it speak for itself.

****

As a child, I can remember waking up one night from a horrible nightmare to find my father standing over my bed. In the dream, which has reoccurred in one form or another throughout my life, I struggle, trying to fight my way out of a formless, deep, and all-encompassing void. It is a struggle for my very existence. My father, looming above me both calmed and frightened me in the same instant. He loomed down upon me, and in a voice, that was somehow both gentle and powerful, told me not to be afraid, that he was there and would always be so. He told me that everything was alright and to go back to sleep. I went to sleep for a long time.

Part 1 – Beginnings

My reality changes -- when I was a kid growing up in Philadelphia, my whole universe consisted of my father, my neighborhood, and my family, such as it was. Looking back, I can see how I was unable to, or should I say, prevented from seeing a more complete picture of the world. Back then the world was colorless. There was black and white – right and wrong. Shades of gray, the fine subtleties of a situation or relationship just didn't exist, at least not in my house. This worldview, if you will, was brought to me courtesy of my father. He was the sculptor of my reality and he chiseled out only what he felt needed to be seen. To this day, I have never met a man surer of "the way it ought to be" than my father. As I grew into adolescence, I doubt he ever knew how his influence complicated my life. On the other hand, I truly doubt it would have mattered to him one way or the other.

On my twelfth birthday, my father permitted me to see just a bit more of the world; albeit under his tight control. On that day back in 1958, my father took my younger brother Christopher and me to the zoo. As we drove to the zoo, my father grew more and more animated. My father was not normally a talkative sort, so for him to get excited, this was something special indeed. Funny thing is -- I cannot recall my father showing any interest in animals after that day. Riding in the car, Chris and I began to feed off my father's excitement and generate a little interest ourselves. Not that a pair of boys, ages nine and twelve, needed too much help getting excited, but with my father it was best to err on the side of caution. Much to our dismay, the day did not turn out to be all that much fun.

The Philadelphia Zoo was not a thing of beauty, at least, not back in 1958. Things may have changed but I don't get back to Philly much these days, and besides I make it a point not to go to zoos anymore. The zoo's entrance was something out of a gothic horror movie -- not a comforting image for us little fellers, to be sure. The sidewalk curved slowly around from the parking lot until suddenly we faced a twenty-foot-tall black iron gate. The entryway reached even higher into the sky. Perched on top of each side of the entryway were two iron figures. The figures were abstract. But I recall thinking they looked vaguely human in shape.

The inside of the Philadelphia Zoo was no safari park that's for sure. Tight little cages encircled exotic animals from all over the world. I remember looking intensely at the gorilla cage and wondering just what the zookeepers had been thinking when they designed this structure. I was only ten but even I could tell how agitated these poor creatures were and how little anyone seemed to care. There was one gorilla in particular, Ramar, I believe his name was, who looked especially upset. He paced back and forth in his cage, as if hoping against all hope that the cage would magically grow larger the next time he re-traced his steps and growing more and more impatient each time its dimensions remained the same. Ramar was trapped in a world he did not create, could not affect, and did not understand. Looking back on it, I think I understood Ramar's plight very well indeed.

As we walked into the zoo, my father assumed the natural role of tour guide for my brother and me. Apparently, my father had a pre-existing plan for our little adventure, because he strode with purpose from one exhibit area to the next. As we encountered each cage or exhibit, my father would call out to us the name of the animal enclosed within. I remember that he looked intently at each animal, as if trying to read its mind; then and only then, after the intensity of the moment had past, did he slowly repeat the name of the animal and move on directly. I kept on wondering if we were going to be tested later in the day. Needless to say, Chris and I were left disappointed by all the hurrying from spot to spot. We kept waiting for the fun to begin. It never did.

****

The second selection from the book occurs about 20 pages later. In the story, the two young boys have just received a visit from their very engaging and strong-willed Aunt Astrid. Aunt Astrid does her best in her short visit to make an impact on her nephews. We pick up the story as the young protagonist of the book wakes up after a night of story-telling by his Aunt Astrid.

****

Every once in a while, we are permitted to see beyond the din of everyday existence, to perceive into the veil of mystery that surrounds life. Sometimes this happens by design, sometimes by dumb luck, and sometimes we are guided by someone more knowledgeable than ourselves. For better or worse, both my aunt and my father were my guides although in my Aunt's case it was more from afar. Both, I felt, seemed to understand, at some primal level, just what the hell was going on in the world. What's ironic was that their worldviews could not have been more divergent.

I cannot remember all the threads of the story that Aunt Astrid wove for me that night back in 1958, but I know the story contained within its tale all the actions that make life sweet and simple. There were heroes and splendid adventures. There were no real villains except those that the heroes had created out of their own fertile imaginations. It was these imaginary evildoers that had to be overcome by realizing that the evil might just lie inside us and not in the outside world. At the end of her story, she said, everything could be honed down to the Five L's.

She said the greatest gift of all was Life -- the first and most important "L." This precious gift is given to each of us and should never be squandered by just trying to survive. Life is a celebration – fireworks, confetti, streamers, and all. She said we all too often spend too much time trying to figure out who threw the party and why we were invited, instead of just enjoying ourselves.

Of course, since Life is a gift, it begs the question, how can we repay the one who gave us this great gift? Aunt Astrid suggested that we do not have to repay this gift, but while repayment was not required, a rich Life is packed with the kinds of acts that fill the coffers of everyone.

She said that these acts were the remaining Four L's. And while this little word game might sound a bit like something out of Dear Abby, it was tailor made for a twelve-year-old. If something you did could be said to fit into one of these Four Categories, then it was repayment enough. The first of these was Loving. If an action spoke of love or spoke through love then it was headed in the right direction. The second was Learning. When we learn something new, we change the way we see the universe. My Aunt said that when she died, she wanted to be in the midst of Learning something new or the act of Loving someone anew.

The third L was Laughter. Life was filled with thousands of opportunities for fun and laughter, although we are all too often tempted to take our actions and lives as seriously as the evening news.

The last L was for Liberty, and by that she meant that we each have within us the freedom or Liberty to choose our own path – to make choices each and every day that can make a difference in the world. Every day we get to choose – exercising that Liberty wisely was the goal.

That was it. There wasn't anything more elaborate to it than that. It all boiled down to something you could scribble on a napkin, if you were so inclined.

I remember waking up the next morning with a feeling of true exuberance. I wasn't sure I understood everything she had told me but nevertheless it felt as though someone had taken a Fourth of July sparkler and inserted it into my soul. As I walked down the steps, I saw Chris coming out of his room. He seemed to have the same bounce in his step. I can't imagine Aunt Astrid had said the same exact thing to him; he was only nine and would have missed the big picture but nonetheless he did seem overjoyed.

At the kitchen table, Morgan presented us with a large and delicious breakfast. While we could have afforded a cook, Morgan preferred to cook for the family as well and my father also liked the idea of one less person in his home. My father was already seated and halfway through his breakfast and the paper. He gave me a look as if to say, what's gotten into you. Then he remembered that Aunt Astrid had put us to bed last night, and his face hardened and his look became more focused and probing. He waited a few moments, and then told Morgan to take Chris to the car and to wait for me. He told Morgan that I would be along shortly.

"Well?" He said.

My father was not prone to long discursive speech. His questions and statements tended to be short and to the point and in this instance, we both knew what the point surely was.

"What?" I said, praying that he would let it go.

"What did she tell you?" He asked. So much, for prayer, I thought.

"Do I have to talk about it?"

"Yes, you do. I need to know what she told you. It's important. Your aunt might mean well but she tends to go off the deep-end, and I want to make sure she didn't tell you anything crazy or misguided; especially if she said anything about me," he added for emphasis.

"No, she didn't say anything about you." I then proceeded to tell him what she had imparted to me the night before. I'm sure that I didn't give it the flair or panache` that she had but I got the basics across.

As I spoke, I could see this was not going over very well. Even a twelve-year-old could read as much. He put down his fork, which had remained motionless in front of his mouth for the past few minutes, while I had relayed my tale. Apparently, the fork was as apprehensive as I was to get any closer to my father at this particular moment.

I was prepared for just about any response, any that is, except for what he did next. He was calm and relaxed. There were no intense stares, harsh recriminations for Aunt Astrid or orders to forget everything she had said. Instead he quietly put down his fork, and with the same hand patted me on the shoulder.

"That's nice," he said. "However, I must tell you the world operates much differently than how she explained. What happens, for example if your act of love causes someone pain?"

"How can that be?" I asked.

"Well, for example, what if you love someone so much that you end up smothering them. You might end up closing off other parts of their life or even prevent them from living their life as they want. You could unintentionally keep them from developing into a complete person," he explained. "Do you see what I'm talking about?"

"Yeah, I do," thinking that despite the big words I had gotten most of what he said.

"Your aunt's advice is too vague and imprecise. It may sound nice but when you put it to the test, it falls short of being useful. He paused. Now let me give some advice that you can use until the day you die. So, that you'll appreciate it, I'll put it the same way your aunt did. Here are your Father's Five L's of life. Oh, and by the way, I do agree with Aunt Astrid on the first L. Life is truly the greatest gift, and it was a gift *I* was happy to give you."

He sat still for a moment to make sure I was still listening intently. After looking me over a couple of times, he decided that he had my undivided attention, and proceeded with his speech.

"The second L is the Law. Always obey the Law – period, end of story. It is the universal adhesive that holds civilization together. Not only must everyone respect and obey the law but everyone must also be equal before the law. No man is inherently better than another.

The third L is Loyalty, and while it doesn't sound as exquisite a thing as love, it's a darn sight better when you're in real trouble and need help from someone. I've always felt that Love is something you say but loyalty is something you do. There is something profound about being there for someone **no matter what**. It's the **no matter what** that tells the people you're with that you really care.

The fourth one is Logic. There will never be a time in your life when logic will not be helpful, even in matters of the heart. Sometimes you must think very carefully how to act when you are in love.

"Lastly," he said, "never Lie to those with whom you share this world. The truth is one absolute in life. To lie is to show disrespect to those who place their trust in you and it will be your undoing."

With that he nodded to me, arose from the table and walked to his car. Apparently, that was the end of the conversation. It was so nice to have that little chat!

I sat there to ponder over what he said – to try to make sense of it. Now I was really confused because as much as this rang true for me, what Aunt Astrid had said felt right as well. My mind was a pinball machine with ideas bouncing and ricocheting off the flippers of my frontal lobe. Needless to say, it was distracting and a bit noisy in there.

That was the problem with my father, just when you thought you had him figured out, he would surprise you and sometimes in the most marvelous ways. His well thought out and patient words and the obvious concern in his eyes made me feel comforted even though I was intellectually confused. He was not remote and unreachable, he was deeply involved and determined to help steer the rudder in my life's voyage – at least so I believed.

****

Well that's all I am sharing for now. The book is waiting for me. It's not going anywhere!

PART 10

Playing the Back Nine – Life After 45

"There are two kinds of people in this world: those who believe there are two kinds of people in this world and those who are smart enough to know better."
Tom Robbins, *Still Life with Woodpecker*

Gunslinger

At a certain point in your life you start to think about your own personal bucket list. One item on mine was firing a revolver and/or a pistol. Having said that, I am not a big fan of guns. I have no desire to take guns away from the masses but I have no desire to own a gun. It is interesting to note that the Constitution speaks to the concept of a militia in the Second Amendment – A well-regulated militia, being necessary to the security of a free State, the right of the people to keep and bear Arms, shall not be infringed, – and that Hamilton's Federalist paper #29 focuses on a militia, not on the general populace owning guns, but I digress.

While I have no desire to own a gun, I did want to try my hand at shooting one. I called my friend Dan Storck and asked him if he wanted to join me on my bucket list adventure to a gun range near us. Dan said, "yes." By the way, my friend Dan is a true standup guy and one of the few people I would feel comfortable with carrying a gun. He has no desire to do so, but any man who is a dead-ringer for Abe Lincoln is someone you can trust.

Dan and I booked some time at a range and off we went. The range was well run and gave a good safety class before ever letting us touch a gun. They took it very seriously, and I am glad they did. Once you put the gun in your hand you can feel the power of the weapon, and it is intimidating. They allow you to select from a wide array of guns before you go to the shooting range. My first choice was a classic revolver – something like you would see in the old west. Unlike a pistol that you could load a magazine into, a revolver requires you to load each bullet one at a time.

I loaded, aimed, and fired as instructed. The first assault to your senses is the sound. Then there is smoke, and then the smell of sulfur in the air. It is the smell that lingers in an enclosed space. It is the smell of something dangerous. We all know that a gun has power and if it is not handled properly it can kill, but something about holding it in your hand and firing it, plus the smell of sulfur lingering in the air, brings home the sense of danger like nothing else can.

Dan and I shot for about 30 minutes or so. I kept my targets as a reminder of the experience. I shot fairly well, but I am certainly no marksman. I don't know that I would ever do it again, but I am glad I went. Both Dan and I agreed, it was a good bucket list item.

Cable News Blues

I hate cable news programs. I don't care if it is Fox, CNN, MSNBC, etc., I am non-biased in my disdain for cable news programs. Let me cite just a couple examples in the effort to prove how woeful these programs have become:

Breaking News: If ever there was a non-sequitur on today's news programs it is this phrase. Let me break it down for you CNN, if you repeat the same thing *ad nauseam* for 24 hours straight, it is no longer breaking news. I think we can all remember in horror the day of the bombing at the Boston Marathon. That was horrific and breaking news at the time. I will grant you that. If you recall, one of the terrorists hid in a suburban neighborhood for a day or so. Specifically, he hid in a boat that was in someone's backyard. A week or so after the guy was captured, I was waiting for a pizza at a neighborhood restaurant and CNN was on the TV. The FBI decided to bring the boat to a forensic lab for examination. CNN then broke into whatever nonsense they were babbling about to get camera crew to follow the boat as it was towed to the lab. CNN did this with the flashing sign at the bottom left of their screen, "Breaking News." Really? Watching a boat towed to a lab is so-called "Breaking News?" I would hardly even refer to it as news let alone breaking. This is just one example, there are thousands. This lunacy gets reproduced on a daily basis.

Reporting versus Discussing: Somewhere during the last 30 years or so, TV journalism has gone to shit. I wish there was a politer way to phrase it, but I think that pretty much says it all. I know I will sound like an old-timer here, but I remember when the news actually gave you news. The broadcast was filled with these strange things called *facts*. Nowadays, you will typically, hear the announcer give you a 30 second breakdown of a news story and then bring on five "experts" to discuss the subject. These so called "experts" are almost never true experts but simply hacks who will bloviate and pontificate lacking anything really substantive to say on the subject.

Somewhere, in the netherworld Walter Cronkite is weeping.

How High?

Why is it that this book has some of my most embarrassing moments? I really should speak to the author about that. In that regard, we should probably discuss my general apprehension of heights. As I have gotten older it seems I have become more and more uncomfortable with heights. I am not totally phobic but I am far from comfortable in high places.

When Val and I traveled to Israel back in 1990, one of our stops was Masada. Masada looks out over the Dead Sea on the eastern edge of the Judaean Desert. Like many historical sites in the Middle East, the history of Masada isn't crystal clear but the general consensus is that the Romans laid siege to Masada at the end of the First Jewish-Roman War. The siege ended with a Jewish settlement of close to 1,000 people choosing to commit suicide rather than become captives and slaves to the Romans.

To get to top of Masada you can either hike up a trail or take a cable car up. Val and I took the cable car. We disembarked from the cable car, and I climbed the remaining 50 feet or so to the top of the plateau. Once you reach the top, you are about 1,300 feet up from the desert floor. You have a 360-degree view of the desert and the Dead Sea. There is literally nothing to mar your view. It's awe inspiring but for those of us who have some issues with heights, it is also intimidating.

I remember Val moved comfortably to the edge of the plateau. At the edge was a simple pole-chain fence. Each pole stood about four feet tall and about ten feet apart. Linking the poles was a black looped chain. To me, this offered absolutely no comfort. I imagined walking over to the edge and going right over. That fence wasn't stopping anyone from falling over – were they serious? Val called over to me have a look. My insides churned. I was ten feet from the edge and walking over slowly. She said, "Are you coming?"

I said, "I'm getting there. I'm getting there. Don't rush me." I got to the edge, thank you very much, but never felt comfortable. It is hard to soak in the majesty of the view if you are concentrating on your own mortality.

Flash forward to 2015. I was in Chicago for a business trip and the company arranged for a visit to the Sears Tower which is now called the Willis Tower. We took the elevator up to the observation floor (103rd floor), and I was fine. Unfortunately, my co-workers to include the CEO of the company were encouraging me to step out on "The Ledge," which is a glass balcony extending four feet outside the main structure. I was less than thrilled. I couldn't just walk nonchalantly onto "The Ledge," but I also didn't want to totally chicken out. I ended up backing my way onto "The Ledge." I looked down – **big mistake, huge** (if I may borrow a line from Pretty Woman). I looked down some 1,400 feet with seemingly nothing holding me up. I held my breath and waited about 30 seconds. I figured that was enough time to prove I was not a total wimp. Then I got the heck off "The Ledge."

A day or two later we went on a boat ride on the Chicago River, and as we approached the Willis Tower, I looked up and thought to myself, *I must have been out of my fucking mind going out on that ledge.*

But, here is the fascinating and weird thing. I have also taken a flying lesson at a local airport. I went up with an instructor in a tiny, two-seater plan. We were up between 2,000 and 3,000 feet. I flew up there with the instructor and I was not one bit intimated or nervous. No fear, whatsoever. I trusted the plane. I trusted it would stay aloft. I could feel the controls in my hands and see how the plane reacted to my slightest touch. The experience wasn't just free of any fear; it was peaceful and exhilarating. Go figure.

Me next to the plane for my flying lesson –
another bucket list item off the list

Facebook 2016

The following was a bit of a rant I did on Facebook in 2016. For those of you who never saw it, here it is again:

"My apologies in advance for the following rant. But if I don't yell into the abyss, I will go outside and start to howl at the moon. Then the neighbors get all upset and I suspect it will all go downhill from there.

Looking in the Mirror: Just who the heck are we? Just a few headlines from the newspapers are enlightening the last couple of days:

- Supporter charged after sucker-punching protester at North Carolina Rally: The man said: 'We don't know who he is, but we know he's not acting like an American. The next time we see him, we might have to kill him.' I will let those words speak for themselves.
- Fans Cheering for Catholic basketball team shout 'You killed Jesus' to Opposing Players: That is another choice one from today's local paper.
- Presidential Candidates Openly Insult Each Other: Need I say more – we have all seen it
- Racial Tensions Explode at Rallies
- The Hitler-fication of political personalities: Personally, until you start to systematical start to kill millions, let's leave the comparison to Hitler, Stalin, Vlad the Impaler, and Caligula out of our discourse.

This is not a political diatribe but rather a bit of self-reflection. We see this parade of nauseating headlines crawl across the screen each and every day. There are additional headlines out there – go look for yourself – pick others that bother you for their coarseness, their anger, their bigotry, their ignorance. Pick them from the political left or the political right – unfortunately they are there. And I am talking about those actions by Americans, not our enemies or evils committed in other countries. I am talking about our own troubles and misdeeds. My point here is that after these types of incidents, the politician and pundits tell us that 'We are better than this' or 'That's not who we are.' Well is that true? Is this who we are? I am beginning to wonder. Can we be better than this? I think we can. For everyone's sake I certainly hope so. Ok done -- now back to our regularly scheduled program."

Death Does Not Take A Holiday

I've touched on the afterlife a bit in this book, but let's not beat around the bush anymore. I emphatically do not believe in the traditional after-life. I want to emphasize the word "believe." This is what feels right to me. This is what I think. I could be wrong! That is what belief is. It is not hard fact. The dictionary defines belief as ". . . having confidence in the truth, the existence, or the reliability of something, although without absolute proof that one is right in doing so."

What happens when you die? Some people believe there is a physical heaven as depicted in scripture. Some believe in a more amorphous afterlife where the soul lives on but it may not have a physical manifestation. Both beliefs have a common element – the self as we know it goes on. It is comforting to believe in this this concept and part of me is envious of those who hold this belief. I just don't feel that is what happens.

I hold two possibilities in my mind. Option one: dead is dead. There is absolutely nothing. The world existed before I was born and it will continue long after I am gone, period. I knew of nothing before I was born and will know of nothing after I am gone. Some people find this pretty horrific and terrifying. Admittedly, it is not that exactly a warm teddy bear type of thought, but I acknowledge it as a real possibility.

Option two: when we die, the soul goes on but not as an individual. The best way to describe is through analogy. Imagine you are on a small pier overlooking a beautiful lake. You dip your hand down into the lake and pull up a small amount of water. You let slip a small amount of the water onto the pier. It beads on the surface. Imagine each drop of water is an individual, pulled from some unimaginably large collective entity – the Universe if you will. While it sits on the pier, it has form and substance. It possesses its own individuality. Now take that drop of water and place it back into the lake. It loses its individuality, but has not ceased to exist completely. It is now simply part of a larger whole. I kind of think that is a possibility for us after we have shuffled off this mortal coil.

In each of these two instances, individuality is lost. In my case, whatever makes up Brad Center as the individual will be gone, done, history. And if the truth be told, that is what we cling to – our individuality. We want to go on, to continue. However, the concept of the individual separate and distinct from everything and everyone else is a misconception. At the microscopic and certainly at the quantum levels this is hardly true. Our bodies, the sack of skin we identify as ourselves, is in constant flux, with particles flowing in and out of us every second. In this fashion, we are hardly separate and distinct from everything around us. Alfred Whitehead called it the fallacy of misplaced concreteness. My point is, that when we see ourselves as part of something larger when we are alive, we may find the *loss of self* less frightening.

By the way, one last parting thought, the fact that I do not believe in a traditional afterlife does not mean I do not believe in God. Not at all, I just don't think that he/she necessarily must guarantee my immortality for me to believe in him/her.

Taking on the Flavor of Milk

Stephen King wrote the introduction to the book *Stalking the Nightmare* by Harlan Ellison. In his introduction, King recalls how his mother's sayings have infiltrated his own speech and mannerisms and those of his children. One of these adages is that milk always takes the flavor of what sits next to it in the icebox. This is why, King explained, that his introduction to Harlan's book sounded closer to Harlan's writing style than King's own. He had just finished reading Harlan's work and was influenced by his style.

I have found this to be true for me as well. In fact, a few years ago I read *The Last Witchfinder* by James Morrow. The events in the book take place in the late 17th century and Morrow uses some of the phrasing and language of the time.

For a few weeks after I finished the book, I just could not get the 17th century language and phrasing out of my mind. It was like getting a popular song stuck in your head. It just kept popping in there. To cleanse myself, I wrote the following email to a friend about playing some golf the following weekend. My friend considered having me committed as he had no idea what kind of spell I was under. Here is what I sent him. Sometimes I guess the milk can go bad!

I write to you as I have just been informed on some matters of import that I wish to convey to you forthwith. These matters do perchance involve an unexpected and potentially enjoyable opportunity for me to spend time in a manner that for me is both precious and rare. This being time without the obligations heretofore accustomed to a man of a family nature. To wit, my wife and children doth look forward to sometime in the presence of extended family. Hence, I look forward to some leisurely time upon the fields of this fertile land, ensconced in the game called golf. But as coincidence might have it I suspect that I may not wish to spend all said time idly whacking said little ball into thy tin cup. I am told that there is enjoyment in the company of others, albeit strange that one might seek out in others for what might find in one's self? Anyway, mayhap you find that you are also unencumbered, I am suggesting a brief meeting whereby we might both enjoy golfing and enjoy refreshments of both the liquid and solid variety. Through previous correspondence and discussions, I am aware that you find yourself previously committed to certain obligations but should you find yourself free or otherwise unencumbered please forthwith send me correspondence indicating so and we can make arrangements to enjoy said golf and repast and any philosophical musing as we might enjoy.

That's Just Wrong

Recently, Val and I joined our friends Paula and Seth for dinner. There was one other couple invited as well and together we chatted and eventually sat down to dinner. The conversation moved (as they often do with people around the dinner table) from one subject to another without much in the way of a guiding topic. Naturally enough, we got on to the subject of food (we were eating dinner after all) and we all tended to agree that certain food combinations are just wrong. For example, putting mayonnaise on french fries or a hot dog is just wrong. My kids seem to put mayo on everything, and while I have nothing personal against mayo, it does not belong on a hot dog or fries. You put mustard on a hot dog and you put ketchup on your fries – period, that's all. Are we all clear on this? The exception here is my lovely wife who absolutely hates condiments of any kind but we will allow her this one idiosyncrasy.

From there we meandered onto other things that are just wrong like:

- Paying for your groceries with a check is not only wrong it should be a criminal offense at this point
- Leaving Christmas lights up until February or beyond
- Back-to-school ads that begin in June
- Eating a pizza with a knife and fork (worth repeating)
- Cutting in line at a merge area on the highway

There are tons of examples out there but the point is: be your own person and do what feels right. Except, of course, if that behavior is annoying. And yes, you know when it's annoying, so just stop it.

I am Just Saying

Over the years, certain sayings have infiltrated our everyday lexicon in the Center household. Most of these are rather silly, but they have found their place in our common discourse and pop into conversations with friends and family from time to time.

A long time ago, I coined the phrase "You are what you do." I always found it pithy and profound, Val not so much. Basically, the phrase grew out of the concept that regardless of what you say, ultimately you are the accumulation of your deeds. I used it with the kids and others during those moments where I wanted to make a point. Every once and awhile, I even think the kids heard me.

One evening after getting home from work, I was changing into more casual attire and was taking off my socks. I turned to Val and said with a straight face that "socks are the devil's footwear." I am not sure why I said it, I just said it. The phrase stuck and it lives with us now and forever. I have no personal animosity toward socks but they are, apparently, the devil's footwear.

At a bar one night, Val and I were having a conversation, and in the background, we could hear music coming from various loudspeakers around the bar area. The bar was mostly outdoors but we could still hear the music. The music droned on and on. Val paused the conversation for a moment, cocked her head, took a sip of her beer and said, "How long are they going to play this insipid techno-drizzle?" That was the perfect description. It was "techno-drizzle" I could try to elaborate on that statement, but to me this quintessential phrase says it all. Hence, a new phrase was born that night and will occasionally require repeating when such music rears its ugly head.

We have a ton of phrases from movies we both like that occasionally bear repeating. While it has not happened just yet, I am waiting for a serious meeting at work where someone in the room will say something is *inconceivable,* so I can respond with the line from "The Princess

Bride" – "You keep using that word. I do not think it means what you think it means." It hasn't happened yet but I am waiting.

You recall the list of my favorite movies. Remember that I told you that Val and I liked a rather silly little animated film called *The Emperor's New Groove*? From that movie, there is a line where one of the characters says, "Is there anything on this menu not swimming in gravy?" This line pops up periodically at restaurants. Please forgive us at these moments, we simply cannot resist.

Other movies have quotable lines that come up from time to time. Movies like *Ghostbusters*, *Pulp Fiction*, and a bunch of others have great lines, but one that seems to give me great joy is the line from *Scrooged*, "I'm having the weirdest day." Bill Murry's delivery is impeccable in the film, and I find that I seem to have plenty of opportunities to use that line myself.

The Fairfax County School Board and Other Political Stories

I was elected to the Fairfax County School Board in 2003, and served for eight years. I often joked that being elected to the school board was one-step above dog-catcher but in reality it was an important and demanding job. We have more than 185,000 students, 200 schools, and around a $2.5 billion-dollar annual budget.

As a school board member, you are (and technically forever) referred to as the Honorable. That is my official title – the Honorable Brad Center. I received mail at the house to the Honorable Brad Center. Val joked that my ego was big enough already without getting mail so labeled. I concede her point.

Campaigning for the school board in Fairfax is a big deal and it is as if you were running for Congress. You need to raise funds and get your name out there, but more importantly you absolutely must go neighborhood by neighborhood knocking on doors. I recall one hot afternoon in particular. It was hovering around 90 with a lot of sun and humidity. After a couple hours out there, I was drenched in sweat. I was walking by a house and the owner of the house was re-paving his drive-way. He was pouring and spreading asphalt and you could tell the man was exhausted. He paused as I approached. I told him my name and the office I was running for and he said, "You have my vote. Anyone willing to be out here is this heat has my vote." I quickly thanked him and went on my way. He didn't care where I stood on the issues. He didn't care what political party had endorsed me. He just knew that I was willing to go out there on a hot, humid day in August to earn a few votes. He admired that (I assume) because he was out there too and working very hard that day. You never know what will connect with a voter.

One of the goofy things you must do as a politician, even at the level of school board, is participate in local parades. They put you in some convertible and you ride in the parade. There is absolutely nothing for you to do except wave your hand like you're some type of movie star. It all seems goofy and terribly self-absorbed. But you do it. It's what is expected.

One annual event was Springfield Days parade, and there was one year that things did not go as planned. I was riding in a car with my fellow board member, Cathy Belter, when halfway through the parade, the car broke down. I had to jump out of the car and push it to the side of the road so the rest of the parade could pass. At least by jumping out of the car and pushing, I was serving a purpose, compared to waving and generally being self-absorbed.

What I am about to tell you probably means I will never get elected to political office again in my lifetime. But, I feel compelled to be honest with you, my faithful reader. As an elected school board member, you work very closely with the general public. The public may have some concerns about national issues but they pale in comparison to the strong feelings they have over their children's education. You want to rile up a neighborhood, tell them you are considering changing the boundaries of their local schools. You will get hundreds of emails, calls, and letters. There are a host of other issues that drive constituents to contact you, but they always want something – even if it is just time on your calendar. Because every time a constituent contacted me they wanted something, I ended up calling them "constitu-wants." I shared that term with my administrative assistant Kathy and my wife but no one else until now. I am sure the term would not endear me to the general public, but it is the truth.

One avenue for the public to reach the school board was through public meetings. The board would announce in advance the meeting, and people would sign up to speak in front of the board. Each person got three minutes to address the board. The evenings could go on for hours. Board members generally listened but did not respond to individual speakers. One night, we had several speakers address the board and use the same phrase to begin their remarks. They began by reminding us that they were a taxpayer and because of that we needed to not only listen to them but agree with them. At some point, I got tired of hearing the same admonition and I turned to one of the speakers and the audience in general and said,

"Yes, I get it you're a taxpayer. I am a taxpayer too. We are all taxpayers because, guess what, if you're not a taxpayer, you're a felon." It may not have been the most diplomatic response but the audience busted out laughing, so I figured I was safe.

By the way, I always told people who wanted to speak to me that I would be happy to listen to them. But that just because I listened to them did not necessarily mean I completely agreed with their point of view. I would invariably get a call or an email from someone after a vote and they would say, "But I thought you really heard me." I would tell them that I did hear them, but that didn't mean we agreed. In my mind, I would hear the Latin phrase *post hoc ergo propter hoc* echo loudly. The phrase points out the logical fallacy in someone's thinking. In this case, the fallacy is that since I listened to them, I must agree with them. However, I never promised a constituent that I would vote a particular way unless I was dead sure that is what I intended to do.

Near the end of my seventh year on the school board, I knew it was time to step down. I had enjoyed it, and thought I made a difference during my two terms. But, I was getting less and less enjoyment out of it, and I thought some new blood on the board might be good. I started to let people know that I was not running for a third term. Do you know how most people responded? The first thing most people asked me is, "Ok, what are you running for instead?" The assumption was that I was not running for the school board, so I must be seeking higher office. We have grown so jaded in our view of public service and automatically assume that anyone who serves is using that service as a stepping stone to the next office. I am not saying I will never serve again, but I ended public service in 2011 and I have been doing just fine ever since.

Cathy Belter and I at the Springfield Parade before the car gave out.

Ethical Dilemmas

Every year, for the past dozen or so, I go golfing with a group of friends. The foursome (right now) includes Jeff Jasnoff, Rich Kosoff, and Mike DeGeorge (also known as New Mike because he replaced Mike Bratman in our golf outings). Mike Bratman left the group because he suddenly realized that while he likes us, he hates golf!

We each have a role to play on these golf trips. Jeff and I organize the outings and Jeff also identifies the restaurant choices for the trip. Rich takes the pictures during the trip and puts together a photo calendar. I put together various games that we play at dinner and breakfast. They include odd trivia and other fun. Mike DeGeorge does . . . well uh, Mike actually doesn't do anything but show up. We will need to correct that at some point.

Anyway, my job, as I said is coming up with our games for us to play during the trip. Some are trivia-based, but others require some discussion and/or voting. One year, I came up with some little ethical dilemmas for us to ponder over mass amounts of alcohol. The games are fun and they are part of our harmless "guy time." Here are the ethical dilemmas we pondered:

1. You discover a time machine that will let you go back in time and do whatever you want to whomever you want with no significant impact to the current universe you now inhabit. Do you:
    a. Go back in time and make millions by making certain investments or bets (see Back to the Future)
    b. Go back in time and advise your younger self to avoid your biggest regret
    c. Go back and see if you can score with the one girl who got away (now being so much wiser and such)
    d. Don't go back – it's too much work

2. Doctors invent a drug (with no side effects) that will improve one of the following – which would you rather have:
    a. A drug that increases your intellect by 100%
    b. A drug that increases your physical strength 100%

   c.   A drug that increases your sexual prowess 100%

   d.   A drug that increases your emotional intelligence 100%

3.   Your son brings home a date/girl friend to the house for the weekend. He indicates that he likes her but it is nothing serious. She is extremely beautiful and she flirts with you while your son is out of the house. What do you do:

   a.   Nothing – ignore it

   b.   Flirt back but laugh it off as a joke

   c.   Tell your son that his girl is a slut and has some obvious judgment and eyesight issues

   d.   Go as far it will take you (not recommended)

4.   Which one of these would drive you to a divorce?

   a.   Your wife admits to having had several affairs

   b.   Your wife admits to having several affairs and admits this will likely continue

   c.   Your wife goes into a coma and the doctors tell you she will absolutely never wake up

   d.   Your wife empties the bank accounts and 401k or other retirement on some foolish real estate scam and loses everything.

   e.   None – you are the perfect husband and/or an idiot

5.   You run across a real-life genie but this genie does not grant typical wishes (he is a bit of a practical joker.) Rather, he will tell you one Ultimate Truth. He tells you that he will reveal one of the following and the answer will be 100% true/accurate. What truth do you want to know?

   a.   The exact day you will die

   b.   The truth about the existence of God

   c.   Your child(s) future – good or bad

   d.   The truth about the Loch Ness Monster, Big Foot, Alien Visitations, Crop Circles and exactly what is going on in Donald Trump's Head

Some voting questions over the years have been:

1. You believe reality TV shows:
    a.) Demonstrate the obvious decline in American culture
    b.) Accurately reflect today's society
    c.) Are great fun but are over-used
    d.) Reinforce the need to "thin the herd"

2. The Greatest Invention ever was:
    a.) The Printing Press
    b.) The flush toilet
    c.) The phone
    d.) The Spork!!!
    e.) The computer

3. Which of these is the best overall musical album:
    a.) Abbey Road
    b.) Dark Side of the Moon
    c.) Boston (first album)
    d.) Born to Run
    e.) Thriller
    f.) Hotel California

(Obviously, the answer to each is D)

Once, we used the March Madness bracket concept to vote for our favorite TV shows (comedy, drama, variety show, and serial drama). I believe "Seinfeld" won for comedy and "SNL" (the early years) for best variety show. I believe "Star Trek" or "St. Elsewhere" won for best drama and "The Soprano's" just beat out "Homeland" and "Game of Thrones" for best serial drama. I voted for "Game of Thrones."

Bull Riding, Copacabana, and Kenny Rogers

There are a thousand stories I could tell from my golf outings with Jeff, Rich, and Old Mike/New Mike, but the one that tops them all was a night in Scottsdale, Arizona, at a nice resort called the Boulders Resort and Spa. The night began with a recommendation from the concierge to visit a local bar not far from the hotel that he indicated had "hometown" flair.

We pulled up to the bar which seemed like a sprawling ranch that consisted of both an indoor and outdoor bar area and a real bull riding area. The four of us – Jewish guys who grew up in northeast Philadelphia – felt a touch out of place. Needless to say, we did not blend in well. I would estimate that 90% of the guys at the bar had a cowboy hat on. We, most certainly, did not have the required Stetson on our heads. You could say we were a fish out of water but a fish might have blended in better than we did.

We had a couple of beers, watched the bull riding, and tried not look anyone directly in the eye. Rich and Jeff kept asking me if I had their backs. I said sure, figuring I could handle one or two of these cowboys, but if things got really out of hand, we were toast. Burnt toast. I didn't tell the guys that – let them have their false sense of security. Fortunately, nothing bad happened and we got to watch some real bull riding. Now, I am no expert on bull riding but either these cowboys were not very good or there were some very tough bulls because not one of those cowboys lasted more than four or five seconds – not one.

We drove back to the hotel. Mike Bratman was kind of tired and went to sleep while Richard, Jeff and I went to the lounge for a drink, or two, or three. We sat down and ordered a brandy at Jeff's request. Jeff knows his liquor well. In the lounge a guy was playing the keyboard and singing a few songs. I cannot recall his name but for the sake of this story we will call him Ringo. About five minutes after we sat down, he said he was finishing up for the night. We were incredulous. We had just sat down and ordered a drink. He wasn't Billy Joel or anything, but he was alright. We asked him to play on. Ringo looked at us and then over to the tip jar and then back to us. The meaning was blatantly clear, YOU WANT MUSIC, THEN

FILL THE JAR BOYS. We were in one of those moods and so each of us pulled a $20 bill, put it in the jar and said, "Play on, my friend."

This went on for about 20 minutes or so and then he paused. Again, Ringo said he was calling quits for the night. Again, we protested. He looked at the jar again. We had just finished a couple of high caliber brandies, so we acquiesced. Ringo got another $20 from each us. He had just racked in $120. Not bad for a lounge singer.

At this point, we decided to make things more interesting and approached Ringo and asked, "What have you got that we can all sing?" In addition to the three of us in the lounge, there were perhaps four or five other people and they looked on expectantly. Ringo then coaxed Richard into singing "Copacabana" by Barry Manilow with Ringo accompanying him on keyboard. Why Ringo chose that song, I have no idea. Why Rich agreed to it, I have no idea. Rich can't recall why he did it, he just did it. It was ridiculous. It was hilarious. It was an instant classic and Rich actually did OK.

At this point, Ringo knew he had us, so again he started his protestations. He said, "I really need to pack it in boys." So, we forked up another $20 and Ringo smiled. For those keeping score at home, that's now $180 Ringo had racked in in just over an hour.

At this point we invited the others at the bar up to join us at the keyboards. We did a few more songs from various artists; I seem to recall doing a few Elton John songs. Then, one of the other people in the bar who had joined us asked if we could do Kenny Roger's "The Gambler." None of us liked the song but what the hell, we were game for anything at this point. The guy who requested it knew every word by heart and seemed to be loving it. We sang along as best we could. About 15 minutes later Ringo said it was time to call it a night – really. We let Ringo go. Actually, we let him go with $180 of our money, but we all left the bar with smiles on our faces. It was a great night.

The Consulting Blues

I am 56 and I am Account Executive for a large consulting firm in the Washington D.C. area. Basically, I sell our services to the federal government, but it is not as simple as selling a product like say, a software product. I have to demonstrate to the government that our services, methodologies, and approach are superior as compared to many other firms. I have been in the consulting business for more than 25 years, and as such I have learned to converse in "consultant speak," which means going minutes without uttering a single real word – just acronyms. For example, the following sentence actually makes sense to me and others in my industry:

"I have read the RFP, the T&Cs, and SOW/PWS/SOO and this will require us to find a good 8a and getting a strong TA in place to maximize our ROI. I will check the FAR but I think we should consider a JV or we could look for an SDVOSB."

Now, I could translate the sentence for you but I think it would bore the crap out of you. Outside of consulting world, no one really knows what the heck we are talking about, but that is how we amuse ourselves around here. This is how Washington works or doesn't depending on your point of view.

Lost Soul

About a year ago, I was invited to a Washington National's game. The Nats play in Washington D.C. and while the neighborhood continues to improve there are some areas where it is best not to linger too long at night. The invitation to the game came from a business acquaintance, and I stayed for the first half of the game but decided to make an early exit. I had parked a few blocks away from the stadium and walked to my car. The parking lot was adjacent to some construction, and it was dark and a touch foreboding. The parking lot was, in fact, really a gravel lot that some enterprising individual had turned into parking lot. I proceeded into the lot. Slowly walking out from the darkness appeared a figure. It was an old, haggard man, begging for some change.

We have all come across someone down on their luck and looking for some help, but what I saw that night surpassed anything I had ever seen or expect I will ever see. The person before me was rail thin with threadbare clothing. His face was sunken, his teeth about gone but more than that, his sanity and soul were gone as well. There was nothing left of this individual but a bag of skin where once a person had resided. He was operating on pure instinct. I gave him some money but I doubt he would even know what to do with it. I think his begging was some long-ago habit that his body acted out on impulse but he didn't really seem to know where he was. He was past all physical help.

I looked around. I was alone except for the individual who stood before me who had once been a real person but now was just a vestige of humanity. What tragic circumstances and events could have brought someone to this state, I am not sure. What was his story? I will never know and there seemed to be nothing else I could do. We stared at each other for a minute, both of us alone in the dark. I have no idea what he saw when he looked at me – something wholly alien I presume – or perhaps it was like looking into some dream for him that he could not fully comprehend. The moment ended, and he walked on to whatever fate had in store for him. I went home to my comfortable suburban home but the memory haunts me still.

Clone Wars

Quite recently, Val and I went to a casino that opened in Maryland at National Harbor. We looked around and had a drink or two at one of the outside bars. A casino is basically a casino so there is nothing much to say. Then why, you may ask, am I writing this? Because of the following events.

To gamble at this casino, you first need to obtain a "Club Card." You go to one of the kiosks, enter in your personal information, and it provides you with a card. Unfortunately, I kept getting an error from the machine. I went to the nearby desk for some help. The woman at the desk, asked for my driver's license and a credit card and proceeded to check her system. She frowned, and I wondered what on earth could be problem. So, I asked.

"Is there a problem?'

She looked up and said, "Well, Mr. Center the machine gave you an error massage because of a duplicate entry."

"What's that?" I asked.

"Apparently, there is another person with your exact name and the exact same date of birth out there. The computer is programmed to alert us in such cases and we only provide the Club Card after manually processing the request."

"Wait," I said, "are you telling me that there is someone out there with my exact name who was also born the exact same day as I was in 1961?"

"Yes, that apparently is the case." She looked down at her screen again. "I believe he is in Alaska."

My name is not exactly common to begin with and to have someone out there with both the same name and date or birth struck me as mighty odd. I guess I have a clone out there in Alaska doing God knows what with my name and date of birth. I hope he does not besmirch my/our good name!

Empath

The third season of "Star Trek" included an episode called "The Empath." The episode revolves around a mysterious woman (Gem) from another planet who has the ability to not only feel another's pain, but also to heal that pain. While my wife Valerie doesn't go around healing physical pain, she is as close a manifestation of a true empath as I have ever seen. She has the unique ability to truly feel another's pain. It is, as the saying goes, a gift and a curse.

She can feel another's pain so acutely that it impacts her own physical and emotional condition. As a physical therapist, she can talk to her patients and they understand that she doesn't just hear them but really understands their plight. But this connectedness can drain her. Their pain, to some extent, becomes her pain.

The "Star Trek" episode in question ends when Scotty compares Gem to a pearl of great price. Kirk and Spock look puzzled. Scotty reminds them about the parable of the fisherman who finds a pearl of great price and sells everything he owns to own it. They agree with Scotty that Gem was indeed a pearl of great price. Val is my pearl of great price.

I'm Just Saying – Volume II

I mentioned earlier that I coined the phrase "You are what you do," and I have used that phrase with my sons as a jumping off point for discussions about life. I have always liked the phrase, but as I think on it some more, perhaps there is more that can be said. Yes, we are what we do, but we are also who we love, what we have lost, what we dream, who we admire, what we believe, and who we aspire to be. Yes, I think that might be right. I'm just saying . . .

There You Have It

It took about 65,000 words but there you have it, my life spilled out onto these pages. It has been a great ride but I think for now I am done. I've got to stop somewhere! There are people and stories that I realize did not make it into this book. To those I may have missed, take solace in two ways: 1) just because you did not find a place in the book does not mean you do not have a place in my life; and 2) I think I have enough material for another book down the line, so if you are not in this book, rest assured you will make it in the next one. I can already feel the stories coming to my fingers as I type, so I had better stop now.

By the way, for those keeping score (in reference to the title of this book) God was referenced in the following stories: Uncle Lou; Your Actual Highway Mileage May Vary; Poetry Interlude; Musical Interlude #1; Faith; Fatherhood; Death Does Not Take a Holiday; Ethical Dilemmas; and Clone Wars.

The Gambling Gods were referenced in The Honeymooners. The Golfing Gods were mentioned in Fore! The Poker Gods were referenced in You've Got to Know When to Fold 'Em.

Elephants were mentioned in Fatherhood.

"I have no possessions that are truly my own. I am like a stranger at a rich man's gate. What I have is borrowed, and even my knowledge is nothing but hand-me-downs, and an occasional oddity I pick up by chance and pass on to others like me."

Erich Harth

EPILOGUE: ATLANTIC CITY REVISITED

Warning, if you love simple, happy endings just close the book now. Don't read any further. My darker side resides just below and it is probably easier if you just stop now.

They say that life is but a dream. They also say your life flashes before your eyes before you die. Are either of these things truly possible? I suppose so. Is it possible that my whole life is as solid as cotton candy during an afternoon storm? If that is the case, I offer the following:

I'm 8 or 9, it is hard to say for sure. My family and I are down in Atlantic City on vacation. It is a cloudy day and my father accompanies my brother and I to the hotel pool. It is an indoor pool which is a novelty for us. The pool is sparsely populated, so my brother and I take turns jumping off the diving board into the deep end. My father is watching from the side of the pool, fully clothed (shorts, button down shirt, black socks, sandals — you get the picture). Sidney Center, my dad, is not the epitome of style and fashion. Sidney does his own thing.

I am at the diving board, and I do the traditional cannonball into the deep end. I land and for some reason I open my mouth underwater and swallow too much water. I panic, I cannot breathe. I struggle, I flail. I break the surface, catch a glimpse of the scene and go under again. I see my father starting to rise out of his chair. I also see my brother turn from the ladder while getting out of the pool. They are not going to get to me in time! I again try to struggle to the surface but I am not making it. I go under one last time. Things fade to a grey dull haze. I am dying. I begin to dream. . .

ABOUT THE AUTHOR

Brad Center lives in Northern Virginia with his wife Valerie and his two sons, Jeremy and Peter. They are protected by Maxie the Wonder Dog and kept on their toes by Zebulon the cat from an alien planet. Brad has worked in the federal government, on Capitol Hill, as a consultant, and as an elected official in Fairfax County. His only regret in life is the loss of his 1972 Dodge Charger.

Printed in the United States
By Bookmasters